DOING
MISSIONS

How a Church of Any Size
Can Reach the Nations

SAM MASTERS

CONTENTS

The great enterprise of Christian missions is almost as vast and complicated as the world itself. On every continent and perhaps in every country on the planet, the church of Christ is engaged in the great task of bringing men and women into God's kingdom. While these efforts have been ongoing for more than two thousand years, the pace has accelerated over the last two and a half centuries.

The task is complicated and it's growing ever more complex. There are many thousands of missionaries from many countries supported by a great diversity of denominations, agencies, and local churches. Many overlapping strategies and master plans exist. Techniques and technologies are applied with varying degrees of fruitfulness. Auxiliary activities such as medicine, business, education, social aid are employed in hopes of furthering the kingdom.

Recent technological advances have made new models available. The internet has opened incredible doors, both for sharing the gospel and for staying in communication with workers on the field. And increased air travel has made it possible to send teams for short-term projects to any corner of the world.

Most Christians understand that world missions is at the heart of God's purpose for the church. The question that might be difficult to answer isn't, "Should my church or should I as an individual believer be involved in world missions?" But rather, "How do I or how does my church get involved in an effective way?" I believe this question can best be answered by looking at the New Testament. In spite of all the changes we've seen in the world, the real task of missions remains the same.

New Testament Missions

Every book of the New Testament is a missionary book. While each book has a specific focus, the context is always that of the missionary work of the apostles. Every book was written to advance the missionary cause by sharing the gospel with unbelievers or by strengthening churches planted during the apostles' missionary travels. Paul's letter to the Philippians is a great example. In fact, in this letter, the missionary subtext is so obvious that it provides a helpful model for doing missions in the 21st century.

Amid his missionary efforts, Paul had been imprisoned. While in prison, he wrote to the church at Philippi, a church he had planted (Acts 16). He sent the letter with Epaphroditus, a member of the Philippian church who had been sent to help Paul. He wrote with a number of purposes in mind. He wanted to thank the Philippians for their financial support and to explain why he sent Epaphroditus back so quickly. He also wanted to update them on his current situation and tell them how, in spite of his imprisonment, the work of missions was moving forward in a marvelous way. In addition, he wanted to tell them of his future plans and of his intention of sending a member of his missionary team, Timothy, to them very soon. He also reminded them that they shared in the work of missions with him and that they must love one another and stand firm in the truth of the gospel, even if it meant they suffered as he did.

We can distill a number of principles from this letter—principles that will provide a sound biblical model for missions involvement both as individual believers and local churches. However, in this introduction, I want to emphasize one of the most important: effective missions depends on personal partnerships.

Personal Partnerships

Missions often involves a lot of bureaucratic machinery. Some of this is necessary. How else does a large organization handle an enterprise as complex as sending and caring for families and projects all around the world? But the most effective missionaries are blessed with a strong web of relationships that may certainly include members of the sending agency bureaucracy, but usually extends far beyond in a web of formal and informal relationships.

Let me give you an example. I'm a second generation missionary. I returned to work in the same city as my parents in Córdoba, Argentina. My wife and I began a separate work from my parents, but we obviously had a close relationship with them.

We went out under the same mission board as my parents. We're grateful for the quality of missionary care this board provides. They handle our funds, provide insurance and a number of vital services. Their dealings with us have always been professional and even caring. But we know that we're just one of hundreds of missionary families.

Every year on our birthdays and at Christmas we receive cards in the mail from the mission board. These cards are hand-signed by the director. I assume that he probably takes a chunk of time every year and sits down to sign hundreds of cards. I don't resent this at all. I know it's his way of saying, "You matter to us as an individual." I also realize that, given the number of missionaries the board serves, this is the most we could reasonably expect in personalized attention.

Several years ago my dad passed away on the field. Dad had wanted to be buried in the land the Lord had called him to. Burials in Argentina are usually done from one day to the next, but since people from around Argentina wanted to be there for the funeral, the wake was extended slightly.

My wife and I informed the pastor of our home church in Miami, Florida. The next thing we knew, our pastor,

Russell Johnson, was on an airplane. I have no idea what he must have paid for a last-minute ticket, but he was there for the funeral. He not only ministered to my wife and me, but to my grieving mother.

Our missions agency was very helpful during this time with insurance and legal issues. But our pastor was the one who showed up for my dad's funeral.

The Philippian Model

In this book you'll see a number of influences. For several years I've been studying the life and ministry of William Carey, and I'm convinced he has much to offer contemporary missionaries and churches. I've also had the privilege of knowing and working with other fruitful missionaries. My own dad and others have had a significant influence on the way we approach missions. But foundationally, the apostle Paul's writings have been indispensable. I've been especially drawn to his letter to the Philippians.

Philippians contains profound spiritual and theological truths. But there is nothing coldly academic about it. We see a warm personal relationship between Paul and the believers in the Philippian church. The tone is set when Paul writes, "I thank my God in all my remembrance of you" (Phil. 1:3).

Paul is aware that the Philippians were concerned for him and he wanted them to know that his difficulties had "really served to advance the gospel, so that it has become known throughout the whole imperial guard and to all the rest that my imprisonment is for Christ" (1:12–13).

Paul spoke of the anguish his situation caused him. There is no distant reserve. Paul pours out his heart to his friends: "I am hard pressed between the two. My desire is to depart and be with Christ, for that is far better. But to remain in the flesh is more necessary on your account" (1:23–24). And he sustains this pastoral and personal appeal throughout the entire letter.

Fruitful missions depends on this personal dimension. The web of relationships in missions includes the relations between a missionary and those who support him, whether individuals or churches. When we rely too much on the organizational structure of our sending agencies, a relational distance can open between the senders and the sent.

Paul wrote to the church at Philippi, "I thank my God in all my remembrance of you, always in every prayer of mine for you all making my prayer with joy, because of your partnership in the gospel from the first day until now" (1:4). The word "partnership" in the English Standard Bible translates the Greek word *koinonia*. Some English versions translate "fellowship." I like both translations. Fellowship captures the idea of an affectionate, familial relationship. Partnership captures the idea of a relationship that has a purpose.

Restoring the pivotal role of the local church in world missions provides a number of benefits. We'll see many of these in the course of this book, but for now, let me briefly mention these:

1. It helps reduce missionary attrition.
2. It encourages greater support of missions in the church.
3. It enhances missionary effectiveness on the field.
4. It brings joy to both senders and sent ones.

I especially like the last reason. In Philippians 1:4 we see that Paul expressed the joy the partnership with the church and its people offered him. Throughout the rest of the letter, Paul strives to make it clear that this partnership in the gospel is for their joy as well.

Missions is a partnership and there are many individual roles to play. My prayer is that as you work through this study it'll lead to profound joy—for you and your church as you seek partnerships in the gospel.

Sam Masters
Córdoba, Argentina
March 2019

CHAPTER 1

Defining Our Terms

My family moved to Argentina in 1973 when I was twelve. Our final weeks in the U.S. were frantic as we prepared to leave on a ship that would sail from the port of Houston. We packed everything we owned into two wooden crates to be shipped on the same freighter on which our family of six would sail. There wasn't room for anything but what seemed essential. My mom had a new washer and dryer. My three brothers and I had our bunk beds and the World Book Encyclopedia. And my dad had his tools.

I remember shopping at Sears for those tools. They had to be Craftsman tools because my dad said they were for a lifetime of ministry. Years later, some of those tools would be stolen from my dad's pickup truck, but some can still be found in the gray and red toolbox which has been in the corner of my dad's garage in Argentina since he went to be with the Lord several years ago.

I see my dad as one of the last of a generation of missionaries who can be characterized by the toolboxes they carried to the field. It was a generation of American missionaries who had gone to war in the 1940s and seen the bleeding needs of the world. They weren't the kind to say much, but they believed in getting things done. They were the kind of men who had grown up on farms and ranches, and they knew how to work. And make no mistake, their wives were just as tough.

My dad was actually a bit younger than the first members of that wave. He had been a drill instructor in the Marine Corps between the end of the Korean War and the beginning of the Vietnam War. Nonetheless, he fit in with the get-it-done approach of those families who had gone out in the 1950s and 1960s. I remember dad and a senior missionary putting up a windmill to provide water for a youth camp. We stood around with our hearts in our mouths as dad and the other missionary, an old navy man, wrestled the gearbox to the top of the windmill without the help of a crane.

My dad's generation of missionaries approached the missionary task with the same directness. They knew what missions is and they knew how they thought it should be done. Missions is the task of preaching the gospel of Jesus Christ and planting churches. They argued about methods, but looking back their differing points of view were all of a kind. I remember one disagreement. The first missionaries from our group had started churches in an old streetcar they had moved from one property to another. My dad wanted to begin a church by building a prefabricated wooden house. It's clear the disagreement was over the most practical way of getting the job done. It wasn't a disagreement over the ultimate nature of the task.

My dad's generation of missionaries was practical. They were also hardheaded. And they weren't always easy to get along with—at least this was true of those who lasted on the field. I think it takes a certain level of sanctified pig-headedness to continue many years as a missionary. They weren't always right. They may have been too pragmatic at times, but they had an impact.

This generation of missionaries was committed for life. Some retired back to the States only after their health broke in old age. Others, like my dad, died on the field. I know of one missionary from that generation who died long after retirement age when his tractor rolled over on him while he was working at a youth camp he had built. My dad wanted to be buried on the field, and he is. My mom, nearing eighty, still works with women and children in Argentina. My parents and many others of their generation weren't theorists. Or missiologists. But by God's enabling they built fruitful works.

The world has changed a lot since my parents went to the mission field almost fifty years ago. The Berlin wall fell. We got the internet. Globalization increased. We've seen the rise of Islamic extremism and the accelerating moral decay of Western civilization. Some would argue that these significant changes mean that missions must change. I would agree—but only up to a point. There are undoubtedly many new tools we can apply to the missionary task. Missionaries today might not go to the field with a toolbox full of Craftsman tools, but they will almost certainly carry a laptop.

There have been many changes, but has the essential missionary task changed? I'd argue that it hasn't. In fact, I'd actually say the world itself hasn't changed as much as we think. There have, of course, been some remarkable technological advances, but the social changes we see really represent a reversion to the norm. In many ways, the modern world resembles the world of the first century with its paganism, perversion, superstition, tribalism, and violence. Whatever the case, the world still needs Christ.

What Is Missions?

When my parents went to the field, no one really asked, "What is missions?" Or, "What is a missionary?" My parents were Independent Baptists, and in those circles a missionary was someone who went to a foreign land to preach the gospel and plant churches. As an adult, I began to move in somewhat broader circles, especially those influenced by Reformed theology. But I'm not sure you can improve on my parent's idea about missions.

Over the last few decades, the basic definitions of missions and missionary have been questioned. And new terms have been added to the discussion. For the most part, this broader discussion is helpful. I want to look briefly at four related terms: *mission*, *missions*, *missional*, and *missionary*.

My parents always spoke of *missions* (plural). When I returned to study in the States in the early 1980s, I began to hear people talk of *mission* (singular). At first, I thought it was merely a matter of style, a different way to say the same thing. But I came to understand that *mission* refers to something related but different than *missions*. As in all discussions of this sort, definitions may vary from author to author. But here's how I've come to understand these terms.

Mission (singular)

Mission is an overarching term that includes all of the other terms. It is the big picture. Mission may refer to *missio Dei*: God's mission. This is what God is doing in history; he is carrying out a redemptive plan that was decreed before the ages of time began. God has taken the initiative to build his kingdom and call out a great multitude of people to form the church for the glory of his Son. This mission is global and even cosmic in scale. God is redeeming a new human race, and he'll restore all of creation to flourishing harmony under his lordship.

Of course, these are biblical ideas. We see the concept of *missio Dei* in Paul's letter to the Philippians :

> [T]hough he was in the form of God, did
> not count equality with God a thing to be

5

grasped, but emptied himself, by taking the form of a servant, being born in the likeness of men. And being found in human form, he humbled himself by becoming obedient to the point of death, even death on a cross. Therefore God has highly exalted him and bestowed on him the name that is above every name, so that at the name of Jesus every knee should bow, in heaven and on earth and under the earth, and every tongue confess that Jesus Christ is Lord, to the glory of God the Father. (2:6–11)

This passage gives us a glimpse of the trinitarian ground of *missio Dei* and its outworking in the incarnation. We might take this passage as a definition. By mission we mean *God's purpose worked out in history to redeem a people for himself that acknowledges the lordship of Jesus Christ to the glory of the Father.*

Paul also shows us how the mission of the church flows from the mission of Christ. We're called to adopt the same mindset as Christ. Humility should characterize all of our interactions as a church (Phil. 2:3), and we're to work out our salvation in fear and trembling (v. 12). The result of this God-aided effort is to give the church its distinctive character: we appear as "lights in the world" (v. 15). The mission of God flows into the mission of the church.

So we discover that mission may also refer to the mission

of the church universal. But here again, it's the church's mission on the grandest scale. This usage refers to the reason for the church's existence and its guiding purpose throughout all the ages. Discussions about mission will generally be theological and will use the tools provided by systematic and biblical theology. However, the discussion shouldn't just be theoretical. Our understanding of "missions," "missional," and "missionary" should be derived from our theological understanding of "mission."

Missions (plural)

Where *mission* refers to the big picture, *missions* tends to apply to specific projects carried out by particular churches, agencies or individuals to fulfill the Great Commission. It can refer to a church planting endeavor in India, a Bible translation project in New Guinea, a pastor training program in China, an evangelism blitz in the Philippines, or a theological seminary in Argentina. Discussions of missions imply theological presuppositions about mission. However, these discussions quickly move on to practical considerations of logistics and methodology, and they draw on fields as diverse as cultural studies, linguistics, anthropology, sociology, not to mention even more practical areas such as marketing, data management, statistics, administration, travel, government relations, among others. Here the discussion gets down to nuts and bolts of issues as basic as the difference between 110 volt and 220-volt equipment, or the value of metric socket sets versus standard.

For my parents, missions referred to the work of lifetime missionaries who focused on evangelizing and planting churches in one specific country. There was a grudging admission that missions might be served by auxiliary projects such as health care, or education, but unless an activity contributed to the overarching priority of evangelism and church planting it wasn't considered missions. As missiologist Donald MacGavran writes, "[T]he purpose of missiology is to carry out the Great Commission. Anything other than that may be a good thing to do, but it is not missiology."[1]

In Paul's epistle to the Philippians, we see the work of missions illustrated in Paul's efforts and those of his teammates. The church at Philippi was planted after Paul responded to the concrete guidance of the Holy Spirit in Acts 16. Paul saw a vision of a man from Macedonia saying, "Come over to Macedonia and help us" (Acts 16:9). Notice the historical and geographic specificity of what follows. Missions requires concrete, practical endeavor:

> And when Paul had seen the vision, immediately we sought to go on into Macedonia, concluding that God had called us to preach the gospel to them. So, setting

---

[1] David Hesselgrave, *Paradigms in Conflict* (Grand Rapids, Kregel, 2005), 316.

sail from Troas, we made a direct voyage to Samothrace, and the following day to Neapolis, and from there to Philippi, which is a leading city of the district of Macedonia and a Roman colony. We remained in this city some days. And on the Sabbath day we went outside the gate to the riverside, where we supposed there was a place of prayer, and we sat down and spoke to the women who had come together. (Acts 16:10–13)

What follows is the conversion of Lydia and the planting of the church at Philippi. This passage gives us a glimpse into the nitty-gritty details of missions work. We see Paul's Spirit-led, decision-making process, and the logistics required to travel from one place to the next. We also see how Paul's team set about making contacts for the sake of the gospel. From the letter to the Philippians, we see that Paul worked hard to establish the church in the truth and that the church soon saw themselves as a part of the ongoing task of missions. From Philippi, Paul traveled on to Thessalonica. And the new Philippian church supported him financially and logistically.

In Philippians, we see Paul concerned about two things. First, he's concerned that the church at Philippi be established in its faith and that it live out the full implications of the gospel: "Only let your manner of life be worthy of the gospel of Christ, so that whether I come and see you or am absent, I may hear of you that you are standing firm in one spirit, with one mind striving side by side for the faith of the gospel" (Phil. 1:27). Second, he's concerned about the progress of the gospel itself. He's able to rejoice because his sufferings as a prisoner have resulted in the "advance of the gospel" (1:12; 2:22, 30; 4:3; 4:15). These two things were intimately related. The quality of the fellowship in the church had a direct influence on the effectiveness of its outreach.

Paul identified the spread of the gospel so closely with Christ that to identify with the missionary task was to identify with Christ himself. For example, of Timothy he writes, "I hope in the Lord Jesus to send Timothy to you soon, so that I too may be cheered by news of you. For I have no one like him, who will be genuinely concerned for your welfare. For they all seek their own interests, not those of Jesus Christ. But you know Timothy's proven worth, how as a son with a father he has served with me in the gospel" (2:19–21). Of Epaphroditus he writes, "So receive him in the Lord with all joy, and honor such men, for he nearly died for the work of Christ, risking his life to complete what was lacking in your service to me" (2:29–30).

In Philippians, Paul moves back and forth between the guiding truth of mission theology and the practical work of missions logistics. On the one hand, he speaks of God's mission in the world as revealed in Christ's incarnation. On the other hand, he commends the church for sending Epaphroditus who got sick when he brought an offering to help Paul.

So missions is the practical work of preaching Christ, and its goal is the advance of the gospel and the building up of the church. We see in Philippians that missions is the defense and confirmation of the gospel (1:7); the holding fast or holding out the word of life (Phil. 2:16); identified with the cross of Christ (3:14). All of these elements come together in Paul's articulation of high Christology (2:5–11): we preach the cross, build the church, and defend the gospel because Jesus Christ is Lord. Paul has dedicated his life to the hard work of advancing this gospel of Christ, and in the Philippians, he has found faithful partners (1:5; 4:15).

In many ways, the work of missions hasn't changed much in 2,000 years. As I write this, I've just returned from a two-week trip to northern Argentina. We drove 1,000 kilometers and stayed the night in the city of Salta. The next day we went up into the Andes and spent a few days with church planters from our church in Córdoba who've been working in Cachi for several years. We ministered to the people, and then we traveled to Tucumán, about 600 kilometers north of Córdoba for the graduation of students from our seminary. The next weekend we were in La Rinconada, in the north part of the province of Córdoba. We had a great weekend with the church planters sent out from our church in Córdoba who've been working now for some years in primitive conditions. This week our church in Cordoba has mobilized on their behalf because they brought their daughter to Córdoba after a scorpion stung her. She received treatment and is fine now. In other words, the work of day-to-day missions. Specific places with particular people and the specific issues of travel, logistics, and problems to overcome.

So to sum up, what is missions? *Missions is fulfilling the Great Commission by crossing cultural and geographical barriers to preach the gospel of Jesus Christ and disciple believers with the goal of planting new churches.*[2] We'll look more at the various elements of this definition as we progress.

What Is a Missionary?

What comes to mind when you think of a missionary? Nate Saint and Jim Elliot landing their Piper Cub on a sandbar in the jungle? Or maybe a slightly raggedy family in a second-hand van waiting in your church's parking lot?

Outside the context of evangelicalism, missionaries don't have a great reputation. In some parts of the world today, they're viewed as agents of colonialism or as destroyers of indigenous cultures. Even as spies. But I'm not sure missionaries have ever enjoyed much social prestige. In William Carey's[3] day, the members of his team were ridiculed as "a nest of mechanics," a reference to laborers of low social status. The apostle Paul was vilified by Jews, Gentiles, and even some who claimed to be Christians. Paul and his teammates

---

[2] I snuck in the language about "crossing cultural and geographic barriers" without support. I'll get to that in chapter 2.

[3] William Carey (1761–1834) was a Particular Baptist Pastor who was instrumental in the founding of the first Baptist missionary society. His writings and ministry in India played a seminal role in modern missions.

were dragged before the authorities in Thessalonica and called "those who have turned the world upside down" (Acts 17:6). This wasn't meant as a compliment.

Even within evangelicalism missionaries aren't always held in high esteem. They're sometimes seen as people looking for a handout or as guys who couldn't quite make it in the "big leagues" of stateside ministry. Not everyone moves effortlessly between the dusty streets of the neediest parts of the world and the corporate boardroom environment of U.S. mission committees. The result is that the best fundraisers aren't always the best missionaries and vice-a-versa.

How do we define the word "missionary"? Obviously, we need to go to the Bible. But part of the problem is that "missionary" isn't found in Scripture. Of course, the word Trinity also isn't in the Bible, but it's valuable because it captures an important biblical concept. We might begin by suggesting that a missionary is someone who carries out the Great Commission. This gets us a little closer, but not all the way there, because the Great Commission was given to the entire church. Can we find missionaries, in a more restrictive sense, in the New Testament?

The answer is yes. *Missionary* is more or less equivalent to the word *apostle*. Now, this suggestion might set off alarm bells for evangelicals who are committed to the authority and sufficiency of Scripture. This is because we understand that the original apostles played a unique and authoritative role in the history of the church. The apostles were eyewitnesses of the glory of the resurrected Christ, and they were given a unique role. As evangelicals, we understand the importance of protecting the biblical canon that was the product of this unique authority.

However, just as the apostles set the pattern for church teaching by the production of the New Testament, they also set the pattern for the church's expansion by the example of their missionary practice. The word *apostle* can mean a messenger or an envoy. In the New Testament the word refers to one who proclaimed the gospel.[4] Its etymology gives us a useful hint: one who is sent out. Of course, a good rule of thumb is that actual usage determines meaning.

In the Greek New Testament we find the word *apostolos* used not just to describe the original twelve apostles, but of others as well who shared in gospel work. Paul refers to Epaphroditus as an apostle (Phil. 2:25). Epaphroditus had been sent on a mission by the church to help Paul. In 2 Corinthians we find that Paul refers to a group of brothers as apostles in 8:23. These men had been appointed by the churches to raise funds to aid the suffering Christians in Jerusalem. We also see in this chapter a reference to Titus who had been appointed by the churches to travel with Paul in this work (2 Cor. 8:19).

So we see that *apostle* can refer to the twelve apostles and their unique office—we can call the Apostles with a capital "A." It can also refer or to others who shared in the task of spreading the gospel—apostles with a small "a." The

---

[4] See the Bauer-Danker Greek Lexicon of the New Testament (BDAG).

word *missionary* serves as a more or less equivalent term for apostle with a small "a."

So what did these missionaries—these fellow workers of the apostles—actually do? Maybe the first thing we should note is that the missionaries were appointed by the churches and as such were representatives of those churches. We see this in Acts 13 when Paul and Barnabas were sent on their first missionary journey. We also see this in 2 Corinthians where Paul makes it clear that Titus had been appointed by the churches (8:19), as well as the envoys who were collecting the offering for Jerusalem (8:23). We know that Timothy joined Paul's apostolic team at the recommendation of the church.

The second thing we might note is that the basic function of these missionaries was more or less the same as that of Paul. Their commission may have been to a specific task like that of Epaphroditus, or like the men who collected the offering in 2 Corinthians 8. Or it may have been to form part of an apostolic team on a long-term basis. Whatever the case, while they didn't enjoy Paul's unique authority, they were involved in the same great task. In a word, they preached the gospel and established and strengthened churches.

So, a missionary is *an envoy of a local church sent out to further that church's concrete efforts to fulfill the Great Commission by crossing cultural and geographical barriers to preach the gospel of Jesus Christ and disciple believers with the goal of planting new churches.*

Missional

Will anyone get mad if I say being *missional* isn't the same as being a *missionary*? It's being *like* a missionary, but it's not the same as actually being a missionary. As I understand it, missional means adopting a missionary perspective about one's own Western culture.[5] This is a positive idea. For local churches and church planters working in their culture, it means looking at the surrounding culture and seeing the needs of the community and the cultural barriers to the gospel, and then taking steps to minimize those barriers. Local churches become their own micro-cultures. While this is often good, it can also be an impediment to the gospel. We must take into account Western civilization's transition to a post-Christian stage. Missional means studying our local community as a missionary would on a foreign field and looking for places where a bridge can be built for the sake of the gospel.

Being missional is critically important, but it's not the same as being a missionary. Perhaps the two words can be placed on a spectrum. A missionary is someone who is sent. So a missionary goes somewhere. Going somewhere means crossing barriers of geography, culture, and language. Missional might be defined as *the adoption of*

---

[5] Lesslie Newbigin's thinking has been seminal on the missional nature of the church. His book, *The Open Secret: An Introduction to the Theology of Mission*, rev. ed. (Grand Rapids: Eerdmans, 1995), would be a good place to start.

a missionary mindset and methods by European or North American churches to reach a Western culture that has entered a post-Christian era. It's possible to do this while not actually crossing any significant barriers other than the natural difference between the culture of the local church and that of the surrounding community. In other words, doing ministry in one's own place, language, and culture. Again, this is a good thing. In fact, it's vitally important. It's just not the same as being a missionary.

Being a missional church is an especially good thing if it leads us to the next step of being a missions sending church. I could go on a little rant here about things like an over-reliance on Starbucks coffee in the lobby and contemporary music in worship. But the fact is, I actually like coffee in the lobby[6] and contemporary music as long it's theologically rich and occupies its proper place. What's more, if you're reading this, I suspect you're already interested in more than tweaking the culture of your church to be effective in reaching your local community.

I'm actually more concerned about a sad irony of missions. In the two hundred plus year history of modern missions one of the shortfalls has been that we often fail to teach churches on the field—to be self-supporting, self-governing, and self-replicating. In other words, as missionaries we've often failed not in planting churches but in planting *missionary* churches. We've taught the people personal evangelism, but we haven't made it clear that the Great Commission is

---

[6] Maybe not Starbucks, but that's a different matter.

also incumbent on them. So everything in this book is for me. I don't want to plant churches on the mission field that don't have their own missionary vision.

CHAPTER 2

Looking More Closely at Missions

When people visit us in Argentina from the United States, I like to take them on a walking tour of the city of Córdoba. Before we set out, we look at the city on Google Earth. It's great because you can zoom out and see the whole world and then zoom in to see the city in ever tighter contexts: the Western hemisphere, South America, Argentina, the province of Córdoba, and all the way down to the twenty blocks that are between our house and the church. In this chapter we're going to do something similar. Earlier we surveyed various terms associated with missions: mission, missions, missionary, and missional. Now we want to zoom in on the meaning of *missions*. We offered this definition: *Missions is fulfilling the Great Commission by crossing cultural and geographical barriers to preach the gospel of Jesus Christ and disciple believers with a goal of planting new churches.* What does this mean for your local church?

Missions Requires Global Efforts

When we talk about missions there is always the temptation to ask, "Why, when we have so many needs at home, do we insist on doing missions in foreign countries?" In the United States, the needs of local communities are more than enough to tax the resources of our churches. Now, I'm convinced of the need for a certain level of sanctified practicality about missions; we have to be wise in the use of the resources the Lord provides. So why the insistence on global missions? Quite simply, because it's what the Lord commands (Matt. 28:18–20).

We can identify various motivations for world missions. Philippians 2 makes it clear that the ultimate purpose of missions is to bring glory to the Father through the Son. Compassion for the lost is another legitimate motivation. And no, this isn't incompatible with the other motivations. We can say it's legitimate to do missions for God's glory, and out of compassion for the lost. But the most straightforward reason is that, for the church, missions represents the marching orders we have received from Christ. In this chapter I want to look at an essential aspect of the missionary command: it's an international and cross-cultural imperative. These two elements of the missionary command are so closely linked that it's difficult to separate them entirely.

Missions Is International

In Romans 15:20 Paul writes, "and thus I make it my

ambition to preach the gospel, not where Christ has already been named, lest I build on someone else's foundation." His desire to not build on another's foundation is probably due in part to a desire to avoid conflict and to defend the validity of his own apostleship, which was at times contested. Nonetheless, it had the effect—and surely this was part of Paul's motivation as well—of pushing the boundaries of evangelized territories ever outwards.

Acts 17:30 can be taken as a key passage for understanding Paul's missionary ministry. This passage contains Paul's famous sermon to the Athenians on Mars Hill. It gives us a great example of contextualization of the gospel message. This passage is also useful in defining the missionary task. Paul declares, "The times of ignorance God overlooked, but now he commands all people everywhere to repent" (v. 30). This verse gives us an alternative definition of missions: *Missions is the task of telling all people in all places that God has commanded them to repent.* It's essentially the same as the one we suggested above, but I like the directness it derives from Paul's statement.

There was a time for Americans when the international and cross-cultural aspects of missions lined up neatly. When Adoniram Judson went to Burma in 1812 there was no thought of Burmese people coming to America. Of course, that is no longer the case.[7] The mission field has come to American

---

[7] Even at this time, it should be said, Adoniram Judson's mission had been preceded by many attempts by New England Puritan's to reach the various tribes of Indians. But you get my point.

shores. According to *U.S. News and World Report,* in 2016 the U.S. accepted 1,183,500 permanent legal migrants.[8] This brought the entire U.S. foreign-born population to more than 13 percent of the total population. But for the sake of clarity, let's look first at the international element of missions.

The various iterations of the Great Commission in the New Testament make it clear the missionary task is a world-wide endeavor. In Matthew 28:19 Jesus says that we're to make disciples of "all nations." In Mark 16:15 we're told to "go into all the world and proclaim the gospel to the whole creation." In Acts 1:8, Jesus tells his disciples, "you will be my witnesses in Jerusalem, and in all Judea and Samaria, and to the end of the earth."

The Great Commission can be seen as the recapitulation of what theologians call the cultural mandate. In Genesis 1:28, God tells Adam and Eve to be fruitful and to multiply and to exercise dominion over the earth. Man was to do this as God's representative in the created order. The fall played havoc with this imperative. Now, however, through missions outreach, we once again proclaim the universal Lordship of Christ, the second Adam. He's Lord of all of creation and over all peoples and we've been commissioned to declare salvation in his name.

One way to understand the book of Acts is to see it as the account of how Acts 1:8—where Jesus declares to

---

[8] Gaby Galvin, "10 Countries That Take the Most Immigrants," *U.S. News and World Report,* July 3, 2018, https://www.usnews.com/news/slideshows/10-countries-that-take-the-most-immigrants

his disciples, "But you will receive power when the Holy Spirit has come upon you, and you will be my witnesses in Jerusalem and in all Judea and Samaria, and to the end of the earth"—was worked out in the life of the early church. Acts then describes the initial spread of the gospel from the church at Jerusalem. Representatives of the church such as Peter, Stephen, and Philip preached the gospel, first in Jerusalem, and then in Judea and Samaria. Later in the book, as the Word continues to spread, the focus shifts to the ministry of Paul and a new center of missionary expansion from the church at Antioch. Our book of Philippians catches Paul at one stage of this outward expansion. The church at Philippi was the first church planted on the European continent. Working south, using Philippi as a new base, Paul planted churches in many other cities of the Greek peninsula.

God is concerned to spread the glory of his name to every corner of creation. The gospel by its very nature overcomes geographic, cultural, and language barriers. The Great Commission requires the church to disciple the nations. This reference to the nations implies overcoming both cultural and geographic obstacles. To make this clear, Christ got specific. You'll be witnesses to me in Jerusalem, Judea, Samaria, and the uttermost parts of the earth. We can continue to add place names to that list. The gospel must be carried to the next place down the road. From Jerusalem to Antioch to the many cities of Asia Minor to Philippi, Athens, Corinth, Rome, the Iberian Peninsula, Northern Europe, the British

Isles, North America, Argentina, and onward until there are no more stops on the road and Jesus returns.

The Challenge and Opportunity of Globalization

During our own times, the process of globalization has made the world increasingly complex. Yet, I'm not sure our world is more complex than Paul's. In the first century, there was considerable movement of peoples within the Roman Empire. Greeks visited Jerusalem and Jews lived in Alexandria and Rome. In every city Paul visited he could usually find a Jewish synagogue. Maybe our present world is more complex than 200 years ago at the beginning of the modern missionary movement. Yet even then globalization was a force. In fact, it was the globalization produced by European trade and colonialism that initially opened the doors for the growth of modern missions.

Now, because of globalization the "mission field" has come to what were initially sending countries. London, for example, has large concentrations of peoples from former colonies. In the U.S., many major cities have growing communities of economic or political refugees from other countries. The result is that when we say missions is to all peoples in all places, it becomes clear that the various peoples of the world are no longer neatly organized in their countries of origin.

So would it be legitimate to say that missions includes reaching out to, say, the Nepali refugee community in

Kansas City? The answer, of course, must be yes. However, here's the key: It must not be "yes" to the exclusion of a strategy that would leverage contact with Nepalis in Kansas City into missions outreach to their extended families who remain in Nepal. My point is that missions shouldn't lose sight of the geographic dimension, even in our globalized world. Missions is international.

While the great migrations of the late 20th and early 21st centuries have scrambled the maps of the world, diaspora missions has created unique opportunities for reaching peoples who live in countries difficult for traditional missionaries to access. For example, I'm currently aware of some excellent projects working with Iranian refugees in Turkey. Turkey, as such, is difficult to reach with the gospel. Iran even more so. But, paradoxically, for now, there is freedom to work with Iranian refugees in Turkey.

As we struggle to define missions, the geographical progression described in Acts 1:8 is helpful. We're to be witnesses in Jerusalem, Judea, Samaria, and the ends of the earth. A mature missions program will want to do more than merely support a representative missionary or project in places that are more or less equivalent to Jerusalem, Judea, and Samaria in the world. It'll see that there are ways of leveraging interactions at each one of these levels for greater effectiveness in all of them.

The city of Córdoba where I live in Argentina is a bit off the track of massive global migrations. Even so, we draw immigrants from Bolivia, Peru, and most recently, Venezuela.

Right now we have two new Venezuelan families in our church that have fled the chaos in their country. I pray the Lord will bring peace to Venezuela and use those who have been forced to flee to carry the gospel back to their people eventually. I'm also praying for Senegal because Córdoba has received a small influx of refugees from that African country. They're mainly men, and they live in a section of downtown near a small mosque. A member of our church lives near them and has begun to develop friendly relations with some of them. It's the only way I can see to reach them.

Missions Is Cross-cultural

The progression we see in Acts from Judea to the ends of the earth represents not just geographic expansion but cultural as well. Samaritans weren't that far away from Judea in a geographic sense, and there were no significant language barriers. But there was an ethnic and cultural barrier that had to be overcome. Antioch, on the other hand, was much further away, both geographically and culturally, even though it contained a Jewish cultural enclave.

There is a transcultural priority in God's redemptive plan. His purpose isn't just to exercise dominion over every corner of the planet, but also to be praised by people of every culture. If we're careful, we can speak of genuine biblical multiculturalism. This biblical multiculturalism isn't precisely the multiculturalism that is prevalent in many parts of the Western world today. The difference is perhaps analogous to the way it's possible to make a biblical case for the conservation of the environment that will not overlap exactly with secular environmentalism.

God is glorified in diversity. There are many places in Scripture where we can go to demonstrate God's interest in the redemption of people from many cultures, but one of my favorites is Revelation 7:9 which describes that great scene in heaven: "After this I looked, and behold, a great multitude that no one could number, from every nation, from all tribes and peoples and languages, standing before the throne and before the Lamb, clothed in white robes, with palm branches in their hands." This is the end of history—the culmination of God's redemptive plan. Christ is exalted, and a great diversity of peoples are brought into eternal fellowship with the triune God. If you suffer from a twinge of xenophobia, I guess, just get over it.

In this passage, we see social unity and diversity in perfect equilibrium for the first time in the history of our race. I find it interesting that this great diversity is highlighted. It's as if the ethnic, cultural, and linguistic distinctions are preserved as evidence of the magnificence of God's fulsome grace.

The Great Cities Strategy for Reaching the World

The world is a huge place. As we think about the global scope of the Great Commission, it can be overwhelming, and this can lead to paralysis. How can one church or one believer meaningfully contribute? It's helpful to land on a strategy that provides a starting place for engaging in the task. Since the end of the 20th century, many approaches to world mission have emerged. Much emphasis has been put on identifying unreached people groups. A related approach is a focus on the neediest areas of the world which some have identified as the countries within the 10/40 window.[9] Another approach is to reach out to the most isolated tribes of the world. This might overlap with the 10/40 approach, but not entirely. All of these approaches have some value, although I am concerned by a doctrinaire approach taken at times by advocates in support of paradigms that quite honestly depend at times on questionable assumptions.[10]

My preferred approach might be called the Great Cities Strategy. This approach has the advantage of having been modeled by Paul. Sent from a major city, Antioch, he

---

[9] The "10/40 Window" refers to the area of the Northern hemisphere between 10 and 40 degrees of latitude in Africa and Asia that contains a majority of the world's population and some of the neediest countries, both spiritually and economically.

[10] I don't suppose I can make this statement without offering some explanation. Let me just raise some questions for those who are missiologically inclined. To what degree has our definition of *ethne* been derived exegetically from Scripture and to what degree is it a sociological construct imposed on the text? On what biblical basis can we accept the definition of unreached people based on the statistical parameters offered today? What's the proper way to integrate input from the social sciences with the guidance of the Holy Spirit?

concentrated on places like Ephesus that served as major cultural and transportation hubs. Places from which the gospel and the church might spread like a virus. Please note that I don't think that this excludes other perspectives. The ultimate purpose is that the gospel might spread from major hubs to the last node of a cultural or geographic network. I know missionaries who are serving in primitive tribal contexts. I half-jokingly call those people "real missionaries." I wouldn't question their approach or their sacrifice for an instant. Nonetheless, I see great value in the Great Cities Strategy approach.

Let me summarize this approach by sketching a brief history of our work in Argentina. My parents started churches that ministered to the poorer areas of the city. This is a great approach, and it yields eternal fruit. However, I got interested in a slightly different approach. The year I turned seventeen my family moved from Buenos Aires to Córdoba, the second largest city in Argentina. Playing in a neighborhood *fútbol*[11] tournament, I made some friends who were university students. Some were middle class, but not all. What they had in common, besides *fútbol*, was a desire to study. At that time I began to think about the value of a church planted near the university.

In 1997, when we planted our first church, Iglesia Crecer, we began downtown near the University of Córdoba with its 50,000 students. The location offered some advantages. There was greater exposure. The downtown area of Córdoba

---

[11] Soccer, of course.

is vital and full of people, so we were able to hand out many thousands of invitations. The location also made it easy for people from all over the city to reach with public transportation. This allowed us to draw from every area of the city. The result was a church with a cross-section of social classes. We also saw the growth of a strong group of college students.

Since that time we've seen various works planted around the province of Córdoba.[12] Each of these new works has been, in some ways, the result of the original strategic decision to plant near the heart of the largest regional city. Let me give you two examples. Jesús Maria is a prosperous city fifty kilometers to the north of Córdoba. I always thought it would be an excellent place to have a church. I also thought it would be difficult to plant a church in Jesús Maria as an outsider; it would take someone from Jesús Maria itself to make a good start. Several years ago a family from Jesús Maria began to attend our church in the city. They had been hurt as members of a radical neo-Pentecostal congregation, so they were looking for sound doctrinal teaching. They drove the fifty kilometers every Sunday with their two boys, and they also attended a midweek small group. As they healed and grew, they became concerned about their network of friends and family in Jesús Maria and began to bring them as well. They showed real leadership potential, so we took the obvious step of beginning a small group in their home. The husband began taking courses in our seminary,

---

[12] Córdoba is the name of both a province in Argentina and its capital city. Of course, it's named after the city in Spain.

Seminario Bíblico William Carey. The group grew and, long story short, they've planted a congregation with its own rented building and attendance that is getting close to 100.

Here's another example of the value of starting a church in a major city. There was a young woman who sold newspapers in our neighborhood over twenty years ago. We invited her to an evangelistic conference, and she became one of the first converts of the church in Córdoba. She was baptized, and grew, and began to serve in the church. She had a real knack for children's ministries.

This young woman's mother came from La Rinconada, a tiny town in an isolated area in the north part of the province of Córdoba. Before we met her, we didn't even know this place existed. It's at the end of eighty kilometers of dirt road. If it rains, the mud will bury your vehicle up to the axles, and you might be stuck there for a week.

She had family that still lived in La Rinconada, and after a cousin committed suicide, she began to have a real burden for the people. After a time, she married a university student in our church. He also came from a small town and had come to the city to study engineering. As a couple, they began making the trip on the bus to La Rinconada to do evangelistic Bible studies and children's outreach about once a month. They did this for nine years while they studied in the Seminario Carey. During this time, she also earned a teaching degree with a specialization in teaching in small rural schools.

They now lead a work in La Rinconada. The church in

Córdoba built them a small house and a church building with the help of The Crecer Foundation and a couple of great churches from the U.S. that sent teams. Recently, through her work as a teacher in the rural schools, doors have opened in Los Pozos, another small town. Visiting this area around La Rinconada and Los Pozos is like time travel back to when the Gauchos roamed the pampas. In fact, along with ostrich-like ñandú birds (or rheas), the Gauchos are still there. People subsist by herding goats and cattle. In Los Pozos, there is no electricity or telephone service, but Lord willing, they'll have a gospel-preaching church. I don't know if a missiologist would classify these people as an unreached people group, but it was undoubtedly an unevangelized area until this couple began working there.

The churches in Jesús Maria and La Rinconada are both fruit of the Great Cities Strategy. Paul's strategy still works. It's not entirely clear how many churches Paul directly planted during his missionary ministry. What is clear is that his Great Cities Strategy was fruitful. He may have only planted one church in Asia—at Ephesus. But from that church, many others were planted. These daughter churches probably include the seven churches of Asia addressed in the book of Revelation.

It's the nature of great cities that they draw to themselves people from the hinterland. It's also true that, as people emigrate to urban areas, cultural ties that might be a barrier to the gospel are weakened. But those same ties become the links by which the gospel travels back to areas that a gringo missionary might not effectively reach. Here we see the value of a biblical church planted in a cosmopolitan city that welcomes new believers of every economic class and social grouping.[13] Just like in Paul's days, networks of personal relationships provide connections that help the spread of the gospel to every corner of the map.

Missions from Everywhere to Everywhere

The more than two hundred years of evangelical missions efforts have brought us in the last few decades to a new phase. Students of international relations say that our world has passed from a bipolar world before the fall of the Berlin Wall to a multipolar world after a brief period in which the influence of the U.S. created a unipolar context. There have been similar changes in world missions over the last few decades. The modern missionary movement began in Europe and received its first great impetus from Great Britain. During the 19th century, U.S. missionary efforts became prominent. The U.S. continued to play a dominant role well into the second half of the 20th century. However, since the end of the 20th century—and gaining momentum in the 21st century—more and more missionaries are being sent from places once seen primarily as mission fields. This

---

[13] This is one reason I'm not a fan of the homogeneous unit principle approach to church planting. It may be helpful in the early stages of the work, but it limits the church's eventual outreach by reducing the diversity of the cultural networks of its members.

is, of course, one of the best things that could happen to the missionary movement. For one thing, it helps to disentangle the gospel from global politics. It also expands the potential missionary workforce, and it brings in people with unique gifts, perspectives, and callings.

Personally, I'm a big fan of Latin American missionaries. These missionaries are especially well-suited for some of the more difficult fields in the 10/40 window. Latin Americans, for example, tend less towards task orientation and more towards relationship building. This is particularly well-suited for the type of work that needs to be done, for example, among Muslims. North Americans might be surprised to discover the many similarities between Hispanic and Islamic culture. These links are the result of hundreds of years of Islamic occupation of Spain. I don't want to go too far out on a limb, but I don't think that it's a coincidence that a growing concern to reach Islamic nations coincides with a growing missionary impulse among Latin Americans.

Some years ago I visited some Latin American missionaries in a country in the 10/40 window. One of them invited me to visit the soccer ministry he had developed. I went to visit him early morning in a large city park. When I arrived, I found a large group of boys running drills. One group consisted of older teens, while the other group was younger. My friend was working directly with the younger group, and he told them, "I want you to meet my friend from Argentina." The boys were all wearing maroon colored soccer jerseys. When he mentioned Argentina, half of the boys excitedly raised their jerseys to show that underneath they were wearing the blue and white stripes of Argentina's national team. Then they began the traditional chant, "Argentina, Argentina!" I loved it! When they began to yell, immediately, other boys revealed Brazil's yellow jerseys. It was hilarious to see South America's greatest soccer rivalry re-created in that country.

I suppose my friend set this all up. I think he was just having some fun with me, but it made a profound point. South Americans are able to open many doors that North Americans cannot. Let me explain it this way: In most places you might visit around the world, no one would know anything about Tom Brady. But they know about Lionel Messi.

International teams and partnerships are the future of missions. And Americans will not always be the team leaders. Often their roles will be in support ministries. At the same time, it would be a mistake to go to the other extreme seen at times in certain Latin American contexts of excluding leadership just because of their origins in the Northern hemisphere. Paul developed international teams. At no point was he excluded because of his Jewish origin in spite of a strong push to promote Gentile leadership. After all, leadership is a service that, like all other services, should be designated based on spiritual maturity and giftedness. The model must be found in the New Testament, God's blueprint for the church.

There is much that Latin American missionaries (as well as those from South Korea, China, India, the Philippines, to name a few) can teach those of European and North American extraction. At the same time, it's a reality that churches and agencies from the global north have more than 200 years of experience and institutional memory. Not to mention, access to resources not always available in the rest of the world. These resources are not just financial. Ninety percent of the theological training resources are concentrated in the U.S. One of the most important things we can offer is education. This, again, is an area where we shouldn't rely on secular ideologies or worldviews to drive our decision-making process. There might be a fear that we're being colonialists by teaching theology to pastors of the majority world. But let's not fall for the idea that every region or culture needs to develop its own unique theology. While people from different cultural backgrounds will bring uniquely valuable perspectives to the study of theology—and northerners need to be open to the possibility their cultural lenses may have caused them to miss something of importance—in the final analysis, there aren't multiple theologies. There is just one faith "once for all delivered to the saints" (Jude 3). This faith was passed on by theologians such as Paul the Jew, Augustine the African, Calvin the Frenchman, and Jonathan Edwards the colonial American. Their theological insights are the shared legacy of all students of theology and Latin Americans shouldn't be deprived of what is rightly theirs because of the creeping influence of a German economic theorist who spent most of his time in the British Library. Especially given the fact that, if that great legacy is faithfully transmitted, the next Augustine, Calvin, or Edwards might be from Argentina.

Conclusion

One of the most interesting features of the book of Acts is its inconclusive ending. We see Paul at the end of his ministry still involved in ongoing efforts to reach out beyond Rome. It could've had a more satisfying ending in some ways if it closed with Paul's execution. But to have emphasized Paul "finishing the race" might've led to the conclusion the story was about him. It's not. The book of Acts is the story of the work of the Holy Spirit in the church pushing the boundaries of the gospel ever outwards. That story has not ended and will not end until Christ returns. As such, the book remains open to the future, and it includes us in the ongoing story.

Since we first planted Iglesia Crecer in Córdoba, we've wanted to be a church that reaches not only our city but also our province, all of Argentina, and the ends of the earth. By God's grace, we've begun to see that happen. We always repeat the idea that we want to be a biblical church that plants biblical churches in the entire world. This means overcoming both geographic and cultural barriers. In a sense, we're just attempting to ride this new wave of missions from everywhere to everywhere. To do this, we know that it'll take more than our skills, resources, and knowledge. We must build international partnerships. We want to be more than merely missional. We want to be a missions church.

CHAPTER 3

Assigning Ultimate Responsibility in Missions

When our kids still lived with us we noticed that unless a job was specifically assigned to someone, it didn't get done. Is it like that at your house? Dirty dishes could pile up in the sink forever and it just didn't occur to anyone to do something about it until my wife started assigning chores. Of course, even then, things didn't always get done. My jobs still include taking out the trash and yard work. I manage to stay on top of the yard, but my wife often covers for me when I forget to take out the trash.

The same thing can happen with larger responsibilities. Unless we assign clear responsibilities, important things are left undone. When we ask the question, "Who does missions?" the answer might seem obvious at first. Missionaries do missions. However, as we saw earlier, a better answer might be, "The church does missions through its envoys, the missionaries." We could sharpen the point by saying *my local church* is responsible to do missions.

In Paul's letter to the Philippians, we see that the church in that city was part of a missionary process that began when Paul was commissioned by the church at Antioch in Acts 13. In the course of his missionary activity, Paul preached the gospel and the Philippian church was established. When Paul's missionary travels took him on to Thessalonica, the church supported his ministry financially and sent a special emissary to help.

Missiologists often describe missions as a cycle. We'll look at this idea more closely in the next chapter, but for now, we can note that in Paul's outreach to the Philippians we have the simplest version of a missions cycle. The church at Antioch sent a missionary team, which planted a church at Philippi, which sent a missionary team, which planted a church at Thessalonica. This cycle can be described in more sophisticated terms by adding other essential details. For now, however, the critical point is to see the role of local churches in the process. Churches are both the primary means and the primary end of the missionary task.

The Church as End

Why do we say that the church is the primary end of the missionary task? While it's true that God's great redemptive plan brings about the salvation of individuals, Scripture places great emphasis on the corporate dimension.

In Ephesians 5:25, we're told that husbands are to love their wives just "as Christ loved the church and gave himself up for her." Paul understood that his calling as a missionary was to declare Christ in such a way that the church was established. This allowed him to locate his purpose—his mission—in the larger *missio Dei*, the eternal plan of God:

> To me, though I am the very least of all the saints, this grace was given, to preach to the Gentiles the unsearchable riches of Christ, and to bring to light for everyone what is the plan of the mystery hidden for ages in God, who created all things, so that through the church the manifold wisdom of God might now be made known to the rulers and authorities in the heavenly places. (Eph. 3:8–9)

The church is the bride of Christ and the marriage supper of the Lamb marks the glorious culmination of God's great redemptive mission (Eph. 5:25–26; Rev. 19:6–9). The redemption of the church for the Son's glory informs the guiding destiny of all of creation. As a result, the existence of the church becomes a proclamation of the manifold wisdom of God, both now during the present age and for all the ages of eternity.

The Church as Primary Means

The universal church, which consists of the redeemed of all ages, is represented in our days by the many local congregations that have been planted around the world. God's cosmic plan is worked out in the everyday realities of local churches like yours and mine. With all of their warts and flaws, our local churches are embassies of the King and his kingdom. Our local churches play a role in making known the manifold wisdom of God in the here and now. The letter to the Philippian church shows us how this is done.

In the first chapter Paul thanks God for their partnership in the gospel "from the first day until now" (1:5 ESV). This partnership was a good work which God had begun in them. It included caring for Paul while he was in prison and also the actual work of missions which Paul here describes as "the defense and confirmation of the gospel" (v. 8) This partnership included, but went beyond the practical dimension of missions logistics, evangelism, and missionary care.

In what way did the Philippian church play a role in the missionary endeavor that went beyond basic support? Answer: by existing as a visible, tangible example of divine grace in the world. Let me explain it this way. Missiologists speak of *centrifugal* missions and *centripetal* missions. Centrifugal force is one that pushes outward, away from a spinning object, like the force you feel on a merry-go-round. The church is called to centrifugal missions; we're to scatter missionaries around the world. The nation of Israel, on the other hand, was called to centripetal missions. While there are examples of outward-bound missionaries in the Old Testament (think Jonah), Israel's primary function was to be a shining light among the nations. They were to give testimony, by their national life, to the glory of God. By the blessings that accrued to them as a people that worshipped the true God and honored his covenant, Israel provided evidence of the Lord's covenant faithfulness. This attracted other nations to the God of Israel.

In the New Testament, much more emphasis is placed on centrifugal missions, the missionary sending nature of the church. But there is also a significant emphasis placed on the church's centripetal missions. This is because the two are intimately related.

In Philippians, Paul deals with spiritual and character issues in the life of the church. He is building up to a critical point about the churches centripetal mission. First, he pleads with them to get along—to complete his joy by, "being of the same mind, having the same love, being in full accord and of one mind" (2:2). He showed them how this would be possible as they took on the same mind as Christ, "who emptied himself, by taking the form of a servant" (2:7). This self-emptying allowed Christ to fulfill his redemptive mission and it resulted in his exaltation by the Father (2:9).

In a parallel fashion, as the church adopts the same mind of service and mission, "doing everything without grumbling or disputing," the church is seen to be "blameless and innocent, children of God without blemish in the midst of a crooked and twisted generation" (2:15). The result is that we "shine as lights in the world" as we hold "fast to the word of life" (2:16). In other words, Christlike character is the core element in the church's testimony before the world.

The Greek word translated "hold fast" (*epechontes*), is illuminating. It can be translated "hold fast" or "hold forth." Maybe something like "preserve the gospel" and "proclaim the gospel." So in this passage, we see how the practical work of missions partnership is linked to a high Christology expressed in beautifully poetic theological prose. This Christology is then connected to the internal life and character of the church, which in turn is linked to the effectiveness of the church in carrying out the high calling of preserving and proclaiming the gospel in the context of its missions partnership with Paul. In short, it's possible to see both the centripetal and centrifugal nature of the church's mission.

Local Churches Train Missionaries

So we see that to our question of who does missions, the first answer is *the local church does missions*. The second answer is *the local church does missions through its envoys*. It's critical that we understand this relationship. It's the church that has received the Great Commission. And it's the church that is the embodiment of the gospel and the embassy of the kingdom. It's the church that, by the Christlike character of its members, becomes a light in the great darkness. The role of the envoy, the missionary, is to carry that gospel seed in his hand—that light like a glowing ember in his heart.

This is why it's essential that missionaries be raised up and commissioned in healthy biblical churches; churches that not only teach sound doctrine but also live out sound doctrine. Dead orthodoxy may be orthodoxy, but it's still dead. Because of the central role of the church in missions, it's of vital importance that missionaries be discipled and mentored in a healthy church. This is more important than seminary training. Mentoring future missionaries in the context of congregational life is one of the bridges by which a healthy church moves from the centripetal to the centrifugal phase of missions.

Consider a typical trajectory of a missionary's journey to the field. A teen leaves home to go to college. He or she becomes involved in a campus ministry which challenges the student's level of commitment. In the course of the college, the student's commitment to the cause of Christ increases, but at the same time, the connection to the home church grows more distant. Sensing a call to ministry, upon finishing college, the student decides to pursue theological training. While in seminary, the student joins a church in town. In some cases, this church becomes a new spiritual home, but often the primary source of spiritual growth is through the seminary itself. The church may have many seminary students as members, and while it cares for them, the large number makes it difficult to engage in close training and supervision.

Upon graduation from seminary, the student applies to a denominational organization or independent agency. The missions organization provides a salary or, as is often the case, the new missionary must raise personal support from contacts he or she has made along the way. These contacts will be spread out along the path that has brought the new missionary to this point. The original home church may commission the future missionary, but supervision is left to the sending agency.

So, at this point, the new missionary's primary accountability relationships have been with parachurch organizations: the campus ministry, the seminary, and the mission agency. These parachurch organizations play a vital role in preparing a future missionary for the field. They exist because they can provide specialized services that the average local church can't. However, they can't replace the local church in the sending, care, and supervision of missionaries on the field.

Let me give you a counter-example from my own life and preparation for the mission field. As a missionary kid, I was active in my parent's work, and by the time I was nineteen I had helped pastor a small church plant near the city of Córdoba for about a year. When I returned to the U.S. to study, I planned to return to Argentina as soon as possible. Of course, it took much longer than I thought it would. What I didn't realize at the time was how much the Lord still needed to shape my character. I won't explain the whole convoluted path of how we got there, but my wife and

I ended up serving seven years in a church in Miami. It was an Independent Baptist Church with a great heart for missions. While it wasn't Reformed, there was never a problem with my increasingly Reformed leanings, and I was inspired by the missional outlook of the pastor, Russell Johnson, who was also a missionary kid.

Russell was an excellent practical teacher who, on the one hand, often emphasized active missions involvement and, on the other hand, the working out of gospel principles in the day-to-day life of the church. I remember being struck early on by two message series; one on the "one-another "passages in the New Testament, the other on the church in Antioch as the model of a missions sending church.

A particular incident occurred that brought these two emphases together in my heart. During a leaders' meeting of the church, I got up in a fit of righteous indignation and walked out over what I perceived, at the time, to be a doctrinal deviation. I won't go into the embarrassing details. With the benefit of a couple of decades of hindsight, I'll say this: the doctrine in question is one that I still hold and would make a stand on. What I got wrong at the time was how there can be differences of opinion on how doctrine should be applied in the life of the church even where there is a shared commitment to the actual doctrinal point.

I was always a little bookish. While I think I got the abstract doctrinal position right, I failed to grasp that the correct application of doctrine in the church often requires not less theological clarity but more sensitivity to the body.

This became clear to me over the next few days. The pastor did me one of the highest services of my ministry. He showed up at my door and got in my face. He made it clear to me that while my theology might be correct, I had failed to be respectful and loving to my fellow church leaders. I had failed to practice the "one-anothers" of the Pauline epistles. I had demonstrated it was possible to nail proper biblical interpretation and yet fail in following Paul's injunction to "[d]o nothing from selfish ambition or conceit, but in humility count others more significant than yourselves" (Phil. 2:3).

Since the very beginning of the first church we planted in Córdoba, we've had two passages hanging on the wall of our church auditorium. Matthew 9:38 reminds us constantly of our missions priority: "[T]herefore pray earnestly to the Lord of the harvest to send out laborers into his harvest". The other verse has always been the theme verse for our church" "Rather, speaking the truth in love, we are to grow up in every way into him who is the head, into Christ" (Eph. 4:15). In fact, the name of our church Iglesia Crecer (*crecer* is the Spanish verb for growth) is taken from this verse. This passage reminds us of our ultimate purpose and it places truth at the center of that purpose and reminds us that truth without love is distorted.

When I arrived in Miami, I had had some practical church planting experience working with my dad. But I still had much to learn about the nature of a gospel church. During my years in Miami, I became increasingly Reformed in my convictions. Not long after we started our first church in Córdoba, we came across Mark Dever's book, *9 Marks of a Healthy Church*.[14] We found it distilled much of what we had come to see as vital to the church and we began applying the principles outlined in the book, but it was at our church in Miami that I first began to grasp the nature of the church as a body.

Here is my conclusion on the relationship between the local church and the missionary. It's vital that a missionary is sent out by a sending church where he has had significant experience in ministry and has come to understand the church as Christ's body. This understanding must be experiential and not just a theological abstraction. We must first become living letters, "And you show that you are a letter from Christ delivered by us, written not with ink but with the Spirit of the living God, not on tablets of stone but on tablets of human hearts" (2 Cor. 3:3).

Local Churches Send Missionaries

The role of the sending church is vital. Evangelicalism loses one of the most critical elements of missions when churches allow the denomination or the sending agency to usurp their role in the sending process. This isn't to say that missions agencies don't have a role to play. World missions is such a complicated endeavor that these agencies, with their expertise, are absolutely necessary. And as far as I can tell,

---

[14] Mark Dever, *9 Marks of a Healthy Church* (Wheaton, IL: Crossway, 1997).

these agencies want nothing more than to see local churches engage in the missions process.

For now, can I suggest that there's nothing in the Christian life that gives quite as much satisfaction and joy than to give birth to a fruitful missions project? It's like having children or grandchildren. This is why Paul can say, "I think my God upon every remembrance of you." It's why Paul said he labored as if in childbirth (Gal. 4:19). It's really why we exist as churches. Samuel Pearce, a friend of Carey, expressed it well when he said that he longed to be a missionary himself:

> I dreamed that I saw one of the Christian Hindoos. O how I loved him! I long to realize my dream. How pleasant will it be to sit down at the Lord's table with our . . . brethren, and hear Jesus preached in their language. Surely then will come to pass the saying that is written, In Christ there is neither Jew nor Greek, Barbarian, Scythian, bond nor free, all are one in him.[15]

In the last chapter, I mentioned I had recently returned from a trip to northern Argentina where our first church in Córdoba has planted another church in the city of Cachi

---

[15] Andrew Fuller, *Memoirs of the Late Rev. Samuel Pearce, A.M.* (London: J. W. Morris, 1800), 48.

in the Andes mountains. The work began there about ten years ago. It has been tough, but the church planters have stuck it out through some trying times. Cachi is located in a valley between two mountain ranges. It sits at the foot of one of the highest mountains in the Western hemisphere, *El Nevado de Cachi*. The culture in Cachi is different from Córdoba. It's more of a high Andes culture where Córdoba is urban Argentina. Religious belief in Cachi mixes traditional Catholicism with animism and worship of the earth goddess, *La Pachamama*. There has been little gospel witness in this area, and the resistance has been strong at times.

Every year in September the province of Salta celebrates a pilgrimage in honor of the Virgin del Milagro. For several hours, on this last trip, as we drove into the capital city of Salta, we saw an endless procession of pilgrims on the side of the highway. We stayed that night in a hotel in the City of Salta. The central plaza was full of visitors and mass was held in the cathedral late that evening with much ringing of bells. The next morning we left early to head into the mountains to Cachi. On the way up, again we saw crowds of people descending on foot through the canyons to the city we had left behind. We passed many groups carrying banners that identified where they had come from. The largest group, many hundreds strong, was from Cachi.

When we arrived in Cachi, the town was almost deserted. We were told 80 or 90 percent of the people go on the pilgrimage every year. You might think this is a beautiful representation of communal spirit and religious faith. The reality is that, for most, it's a lark. For many, it's a chance to drink. While it does indicate how strongly the town adheres to its traditions, you'd only need to return to Cachi the next week to find men lying drunk again in the streets to know that no lives were changed.

The massive participation in the pilgrimage not only indicates how strongly Cachi adheres to its traditions but also how difficult it is for someone there to break free to follow Christ. The evening we arrived, the church gathered—thirty hard-won adults. On other trips, we had often spent time answering basic questions about the Christian walk. This time the meeting took a different direction. Maybe it was something about the silence that had settled over the nearly empty town. These thirty new believers had made a stand by staying. It takes courage to not walk down the mountain with all of your friends and family—to remain with those who are too young, or too old, or too ill to make the pilgrimage on foot.

That night, we ate *pan casero* (local bread) and sipped mate (Argentina's communal tea), as they shared their testimonies of faith in Christ. Most had endured persecution in school or at work. They told of cold shoulders, hard feelings, deep hurts, bleeding hearts. One young woman in her twenties had been disowned by her parents and had been forced out on the street.

But that night, there was a warmth in that room seemed to make it all right. Some friends from the U.S. were with us that night. They were especially touched. They said something to the effect that while they had always loved our church in Córdoba, they felt a special affection for the group in Cachi that night. I understood it perfectly. I love my children dearly, but my grandchildren melt my heart.

The church planters in Cachi were the first couple sent out of our church in Córdoba. They had an interesting story. He had been converted in a Pentecostal church. Within weeks of his conversion, they asked him to be the pastor, and he accepted. After about a year as the pastor, he came to two conclusions: God was indeed calling him to a life of ministry and he had no idea what he was doing. So he resigned and began to look for a church that would teach him the Bible and how to do ministry. He ended up in our church which was still young at that point.

Not long after joining our church, he asked me to train him for ministry. He also told me he wanted to give all of his time to ministry. I loved the idea of having him work with me, but I had to tell him there was no budget to pay him. He said that wasn't a problem because he and his wife had decided to sell their grocery store and live off of the proceeds. They did this for four years.

Eventually, the church was able to begin paying them. He became my friend and partner in ministry. We would meet in the plaza near our church and walk lap after lap around the block as we prayed for the people and the work. He always told me he loved our church so much he could never see himself leaving.

After ministering in various roles for several years, he

took a group of young people on a missions trip to Cachi. When they returned, he told me they felt the call to start a church in Cachi. Needless to say, their departure left a huge hole. Now we're several years into a church-planting process that hasn't been easy for them or us. We had the help of a church in the Kansas City area that was a great partner in the first years of the project. There have been thousands of kilometers driven, many thousands of dollars spent on construction and evangelism projects. Our people in Córdoba have given and gone and shared in the anguish of the many ups and downs.

Recently, doors opened to have a weekly program on the municipal radio station in Cachi. Slowly, some of the barriers have begun to fall, and over the last couple of years, we've started to see what looks like enduring fruit. That night a few months earlier—when we shared with the thirty new believers—felt like a turning point. It reminded me of when my children were born. There is a special moment after the trauma of delivery. There is that endless night of fear and pain when your wife squeezes your hand so hard you're sure she will crush it, and you don't know what to do except to say silly comforting things and pray. And then the crisis comes, and then the baby comes. And soon you find yourself holding your new child, and you realize that once again God has brought new life into the world.

Missions is much the same. Through the church, God brings new local churches into the world. To be a missionary, or part of a team, whether on the field or as part of the sending church, is a privilege that pays eternal dividends. Seeing people brought to Christ by the Word and Spirit's power, and joined to a new congregation through baptism, is the only thing I can think of that compares to having children of your own.

The Delegated Authority of the Missionary

Earlier we said a missionary is an envoy of a local church sent out to further that church's efforts to fulfill the Great Commission by crossing cultural and geographical barriers to preach the gospel of Jesus Christ and disciple believers with the goal of planting new churches. The missionary is an ordained and commissioned minister who is sent out with authority to preach, baptize, and organize new churches. It's a remarkable level of authority. In the New Testament, we can see this authority not only in Paul's ministry (as we might expect) but in others, like Titus (Titus 1:5).

There are two things we should notice about this authority. First of all, it's a derived or delegated authority. Second, this authority is transitional. It's a delegated authority because it doesn't originate in the missionary himself. In Acts 13 we see that Barnabas and Paul were sent out by the church at the command of the Holy Spirit. So the ultimate authority is actually the Holy Spirit, but it's mediated through the church. As a result, the missionary is accountable to the church that sends him. We see this accountability relationship in the book of Acts when after each missionary tour the missionaries returned to the church at Antioch to give an account of their actions and all that the Holy Spirit had done for them. In our days the issue of accountability can be a little complicated. As missionaries go out under various agencies and perhaps join established teams on the field, lines of authority and accountability can be confusing. But maybe it's no more difficult than how families navigate authority issues with their children as they grow older. We send our kids to school and teach them to be respectful to their teachers. They play sports or join a band where they're also expected to follow their coach or director and cooperate with other team or band members. At the same time, as parents, we maintain ultimate authority. In the same way, local churches and their missionaries must negotiate a variety of relationships without forgetting that only the local church, under the guidance of the Holy Spirit, has the authority to send out a missionary.

The second thing that must be remembered is that the authority of a missionary is transitional. Again, family life provides a helpful analogy. The authority of a parent over a newborn is absolute. Wise parents, however, learn to grant increasing freedom to their children as they grow older. Once our adult children establish their own households, our effective authority comes to an end, even as our children continue to come to us for advice and guidance. The same occurs with a new missions church. As it matures, the wise missionary gradually releases authority as elders are established and the congregation accepts its own responsibilities.

There is a similar progression or evolution in the relationship between a missionary and sending church. A brand-new missionary on the field needs much more hand-holding than a veteran missionary with decades of experience. This doesn't mean that the missionary ever becomes a free agent. It merely recognizes that a missionary who has mastered the language, learned the culture, and demonstrated true fruitfulness on the field need not be micromanaged from halfway around the world. The truth is that the vast distances involved in world missions, even in our age of jet travel and internet connectivity, makes it impractical to micromanage even the junior missionary.

For this reason, the internship phase and the missionary's preparation is critical. The first term on the field isn't the best time to discover a lack of essential character strengths or ministry skills. The mission field can place extreme pressure on a new missionary family. For the sake of those we send, not to mention that of the work, weak areas need to be exposed and strengthened before they produce a catastrophic failure on the field.

The ultimate lines of authority run from the Holy Spirit, through the church, to the missionary. Mature sending churches learn to respect the experience of the missionary, and seasoned missionaries know to welcome the guidance of the sending church. Major decisions need to be taken in coordination with the missions sending agency, but priority should be given to the primary accountability relationship—the relationship between the sending church and their missionary as they both labor *coram Deo*.

Conclusion

Missions isn't meant to be carried out by lone-ranger missionaries. The Great Commission was given, not to individuals, but to the church. The church is both the beginning and the end of the process. Churches fulfill their mission by training and sending representatives with the maturity, experience, and authority to plant new churches that will repeat the process. It's essential that the church, by its very character, reflect the gospel. A new missionary will build a church based on the model where he was discipled. That model must be adapted culturally to the new field, but it will follow the example of the mother church in its character and doctrine. Like its mother, the new church will both hold fast to the truth of the gospel and will hold it out for the world to see.

CHAPTER 4

Grasping the Practical Nature of Missions

The practice of missions is one of those things that may best be learned by observation and participation. That doesn't mean a book can't be helpful. At least I hope not, since this book is about missions. But missions is a bit like building a house. While I'm no expert in construction, I did learn a few helpful things hanging drywall and helping my father-in-law build a couple of houses. The best way to learn to drive nails with a hammer is by grabbing a hammer and driving nails.

Missions is much the same. That is part of the value of a well-planned missions trip or internship. Of course, there is a place for books in the process, just as there is in construction. Most of us want to live in homes built by an experienced contractor, and designed with the help of architects and engineers who've learned the theory. But even the architects and engineers need to get out to the job site and get their boots muddy.

In the next few chapters, we'll talk about getting our missions boots muddy. We'll describe a practical approach to missions that has guided us since we began to work in Argentina. This conversation consists of a lot of borrowed ideas from several sources. By God's grace, these ideas have proven effective and hopefully you can use them as well.

The Practical Side of Missions in Philippians

Missions requires sustained efforts of a practical nature. The book of Philippians and the book of Acts give us glimpses of the practical side of missions. Teams were formed (Acts 20:4). Travel routes by land and sea were chosen (6:10). Passages on ships were purchased (13:13). Communications networks were established (11:1). Epistles and offerings were carried between distant cities (Phil. 4:18). We see the missionaries laying hold of the tools that were available in their cultural setting. They wrote on papyrus, spoke Koine Greek and composed epistles which, as a genre of writing, were a cultural product of the first century. They carried scrolls of the Hebrew Scriptures (some translated into Greek) as they walked Roman roads in route to the next Jewish synagogue or Greek marketplace where they would preach the gospel.

Paul and his team also depended on the hospitality of believers in every city. When Paul wrote that a pastor must be hospitable (1 Tim. 3:2), it was about more than a desirable character trait. The spread of the gospel depended on the practical hospitality of the churches. In Philippians, we see the mission of Epaphroditus who was sent to bring an offering and minister to Paul in practical ways (Phil. 2:30). I always imagine Epaphroditus helping Paul with *tramites* (tra-mee-tays). *Tramites* is a great Spanish word that means errands of a particular kind, usually paperwork and red tape involving the government. This would include things like standing in line at a government office for a bureaucrat to put the right stamp on a document. Many missionaries can tell you how time-absorbing this sort of thing can be in foreign countries.

In 2 Timothy 4:13, we catch a glimpse of the practical side of missions when Paul writes, "When you come, bring the cloak that I left with Carpus at Troas, also the books, and above all the parchments." In other words, logistics matter. They say an army marches on its stomach. Perhaps it's not unspiritual to say this is true of missions as well. If we're to obey the Great Commission, at some point theology must be transformed into concrete action.

A 20th Century Example of Practical Mission

Other than my parents, the two biggest influences on my practical missiology have been William Carey and a Baptist missionary in Peru, Rudy Johnson, who is the father of Russell Johnson, the pastor of our sending church. I first met

Rudy in the mid-1980s when my wife and I moved to Miami to continue our preparation for the mission field. Rudy had gone to Peru in the early 1960s and had a very fruitful work which resulted in scores upon scores of churches planted. Back in the 1980s, before I became a missionary, I asked him on two different occasions the same question. I got two different answers—both were helpful. In all fairness to Rudy, I probably phrased the question differently the second time, which would explain the different response.

The question I asked was to what did he attribute, in a practical sense, the fruitfulness of his work in Peru. The first time he answered that when he returned to the States after his first term, he felt frustrated with an apparent lack of fruitfulness. While on furlough, he read the book *The Master Plan of Evangelism* by Robert Coleman. He said it changed the way he approached missions. The key idea of the book is that Jesus, to reach the world, chose twelve disciples to whom he dedicated most of his time. Reading this book let me see that the most fruitful thing I could do was invest time in potential leaders. (The book is a classic, and if you haven't read it, you should.)

In the 1980s I had the chance to spend time with Coleman when I picked him up at the airport for a speaking engagement he had in Miami. In the car, I told him about Rudy and the great fruit in Peru and the influence of his book. I was curious what he would say, and I was surprised as we drove down I-95 that he made no comment. I thought,

"Does he not care?" Curious, I glanced at him as I dodged traffic and saw tears rolling down his cheeks.

The second time I asked Rudy my question, he gave me this practical answer. He said he saw the need for three organizations. First, a healthy mother church that could be a model and a launching pad for church planting. Second, a Bible institute to train leaders. Third, a construction company to build church buildings. In our work, we've mirrored this approach to a great degree. We began Iglesia Crecer as a model church from which to plant other churches. We then started Seminario Bíblico William Carey to train leaders. However, we haven't started the construction company. That slot is occupied by The Crecer Foundation which works to link partners and resources to evangelistic projects and to build buildings, seminaries, and other infrastructure.

If you think about it, there is an important connection between Rudy's two answers. The first answer emphasizes the importance of raising up national leaders. This is the key to everything. The real key to reaching a country isn't the missionary, but the national preachers and missionaries he trains. In Rudy's second answer, we see the basic infrastructure required to disciple future leaders (the church), train the leaders for ministry (the Bible institute), and to help them move forward after they've done the hard work of planting a church (a construction company to build a building). Later I'll explain how this can be done without creating an unhealthy dependency of the national churches. As we'll see in the next chapter, these are the fundamental elements required to generate an ongoing church planting cycle.

I've heard Rudy say many times, "The water of life is free, but building the pipeline is costly." At first, this struck me as odd, but I've come to agree. Missions is costly in many ways. It requires a significant financial commitment, but more than that, it requires that people give their lives. Sons and daughters must be relinquished to follow where the Lord would lead them. Parents must be left behind. As the years have gone by, it has become clear to me that the idea rings true in another way. The analogy of missions to building a pipeline gets at the practical side of the task. Plans must be drawn up. Tools must be gathered. And the work must be done energetically and persistently.

For some, this point of view may feel wrong. There is a proper aversion in Reformed circles to pragmatism. This springs from our understanding that God is sovereign, and that the gospel and the nature of the church shouldn't be compromised in the pursuit of results. At the same time, we recognize that the Great Commission is an imperative we can't ignore. We also understand that God works through means. So, we face the challenge of working through the difference between pragmatism and practicality. How do we avoid indulging in fleshly activism without falling prey to the opposite danger of inertia in the face of the divine command? If we fail to wrestle with these issues, we run the risk of becoming functional hyper-Calvinists.

There is a great quote attributed to General Omar

Bradley, "Amateurs talk strategy, professionals talk logistics." I certainly wouldn't go so far as to say that amateurs talk theology or missiology. But at some point, if we're obedient, we have to get around to actually taking practical steps. Missions begins with the divine command. It depends on prayer. And it's carried forward through persistent, practical endeavor under the sustaining guidance of the Holy Spirit.

Rudy Johnson was one of those members of the World War II generation of missionaries. He was a Navy veteran, and he never stopped working towards a goal. After a fruitful ministry in Lima, Peru, he came back to the U.S. and among other things planted a Spanish church that would eventually become our sending church. When he was old enough to retire, he returned to Peru to plant a church and build a camp in Cusco. He was almost 90 before anyone could persuade him he should slow down. He had an intuitive, practical understanding of missions that I think lines up well with the missionary example of Carey.

William Carey and Practical Missions

Carey, often called the father of modern missions, understood the importance of the practical side of missions. His influential work, *An Enquiry into the Obligations of Christians, to Use Means for the Conversion of the Heathens*, was an exploration of this idea. Carey built on the theology of Jonathan Edwards and Andrew Fuller. Fuller had taught that faith was a duty for the nonbeliever, and making a free offer of the gospel was the duty of the preacher. Carey took the next step arguing that to carry the gospel beyond the shores of England was a duty as well.

The next question was how? Carey answered, "When he had laid down his life, and taken it up again, he sent forth his disciples to preach the good tidings to every creature, and to endeavor by all possible means to bring over a lost world to God." Carey asked a simple question: If tradesmen can go to the ends of the earth on sailing ships in search of profit, what is keeping the church from fulfilling the Great Commission? God had made specific tools available, and they must be used.

One of my favorite facts about Carey is that he set up the first steam engine ever seen in India. It was a twelve-horse-power engine ordered from Thwaites and Rockwell in Bolton England. It caused quite a stir. The locals gathered around the "machine of fire" and declared that it "equaled the achievements of Vishwu-Kurmu, the architect of the gods." Carey's colleague, Joshua Marshman, was so intrigued by the new machine that he spent three days studying its operation and also researched the history of its origins.

Carey knew that it would be feasible to set up the steam engine because of broader contacts that were the result of his scientific interests. He was acquainted with members of the Asiatick Society, a Calcutta organization similar to the Royal Society that promoted scientific knowledge in Asia. The founder of the society, William Jones, had been interested in the presence of coal in the area and had taken steps to see that it was mined.

Carey wasn't interested in the steam engine as a novelty. It was the solution to a practical problem. The Baptist mission in India had become the world center for the translation of the Bible. Carey and his colleagues translated the Scriptures into many of the languages of India. Joshua Marshman even produced one of the first Chinese translations of the Bible. The missionaries also took upon themselves the printing of Bibles under the supervision of William Ward, a printer and former newspaper publisher. They imported a press and set up their own type foundry to produce typefaces for the many languages they worked with.

The steam engine was brought to solve the problem of providing a reliable supply of paper. Paper imported from England was of good quality, but scarce and expensive. Some paper was produced in India, but it was of inferior quality. It was sized with rice paste and so was eaten by bugs almost as soon as it came off the press. To solve the problem the missionaries set up the entire industrial process required to produce paper. They purchased land for the cultivation of trees to make pulp. They set up a paper mill and like most things in India, it was powered by human effort—forty men pushed a treadmill. However, this came to an end when one of the workers was killed when he fell into the machinery. So, the steam engine was brought to India to power the paper mill.

We could follow the chain of related activities further

and investigate the way the missionaries financed print-ing projects through subscriptions, or examine the trans-lation process that went far beyond the stereotype of Carey working alone with a single Indian scholar. He actually worked with many experts in Sanskrit and other languages at Serampore and Fort William College where he taught, and he supervised an editorial process that would rival any major modern publisher.

John Clark Marshman, the son of Joshua and Hannah Marshman, grew up at the mission. He wrote that the "erec-tion of this engine was in strict subordination to the objects of the mission." This statement could be extended to all of the related efforts. The actual objects of the mission are often overlooked in works on Carey. His achievements in other fields were so remarkable that they can distract from the core endeavors of preaching the cross and planting churches. The missionaries saw all of their activities, including translation and education, as auxiliary to the primary task of preaching the gospel of Christ and planting churches.

William Carey's Theology of Practical Missions

Carey's life work can be summed up as an affirmative answer to the question implied by the title of his famous work: *Are Christians obligated to use means for the conver-sion of the heathen?* He was the embodiment of his famous slogan, "Attempt great things for God. Expect great things from God." Carey's mind moved naturally from theology to practice. His genius was to envision the practical steps required to make the move from orthodoxy to orthopraxis—from sound doctrine to sound practice.

Carey's friend, Andrew Fuller, the first secretary of the Particular Baptist Missionary Society and pastor of the church in Kettering, was the theologian of the modern missionary movement. Over the years he also thought deeply about the use of means. The development of his thinking can be traced in sermons he preached. In 1791, before the birth of the mission society, he delivered a message at a meeting of the Northamptonshire Association titled *The Pernicious Influence of Delay in Religious Matters*. He challenged his fellow pastors, "We pray for the conversion and salvation of the world, and yet neglect the ordinary means by which those ends have been used to be accomplished."

Twenty-three years later, in another message, Fuller was still working out his theology of means: "If it be the design of God to diffuse the knowledge of himself over the earth in these last days, it might be expected that suitable means and instruments would be employed to accomplish it." He went on to use the example of Bezaleel and Aholiab who were given the wisdom to build the tabernacle (cf. Ex. 31:12–17). Then Fuller made application to his own times. Like Carey, Fuller saw "means" as encompassing more than technology. It included organizational structures—parachurch institutions—as well. He wrote, "It might be expected, supposing a great work designed to be accomplished, that societies would be formed, some to translate the sacred Scriptures into the languages of the nations, some to give them circulation, some to scatter tracts which shall impress their leading principles, some to preach the gospel, and some to teach the rising generation to read and write."

Carey's and Fuller's view of the use of practical means was reinforced by a robust doctrine of divine providence. In opposition to the deists of the period, they believed that God was active in world history. This conviction that God governs his world providentially, led to the conclusion that the grasping of available means wasn't just an option, but a responsibility.

Carey didn't hesitate to lay hold of the technological, financial, and organizational tools that were available in his day. The results were the conversion of thousands and the establishment of many congregations across the Indian sub-continent. Carey and his colleagues also had a lasting influence on Indian culture, and their example encouraged the largest missionary movement in the history of the church.

Continuing Challenge

As the confessional and spiritual heirs of Carey, our challenge is similar. We have tools available that Carey couldn't have dreamed of. I wonder what he might've accomplished had he been able to work with computers, Bible programs with tagged texts in Hebrew and Greek, the internet, online educational platforms, to name a few. I'm convinced he would've seen the value of ebooks for theological education.

Carey never lost sight of his biblical priorities. He dedicated his life to the preaching of the gospel, the translation of the Scriptures into the Indian vernaculars, the planting of churches, and the education of national leaders. These priorities are as old as the New Testament church itself. But he audaciously grasped every new tool available to carry them out. While the world has changed in many ways since the early days of the modern missionary movement, our responsibility is no different than Carey's. The water of life is still free, and building the pipeline is still costly. We must take it to drought-stricken parts of the world by the most effective means we can find.

CHAPTER 5

Starting the Missions Cycle

often hear second- and third-hand stories about missions that make me skeptical.

Several years ago, some of the young people in our church told me a story they heard at a missions mobilization conference. I may have some of the details wrong, but the general idea was that a young person had received a vision from God that he was supposed to buy Bibles to smuggle into Iran. He purchased the Bibles and took a train. He managed to make it past border controls, and he arrived in one of the major cities city. There he was guided by the Spirit to knock on the door of a specific house. The owners of the house opened the door and informed him that they had been waiting for him and the Bibles because they too had received visions from the Lord.

While this story is inspiring in a way, even if it's true, it's not an adequate model for missions involvement. It's a great adventure, but it isn't real missions. To be honest, it concerns me since it inspired our young people without giving them a realistic idea of how to actually get involved in missions. Missions is the most worthwhile thing we can do in the universe. There are great moments of joy and occasional episodes of high adventure, but it's mainly tedious work. As such, it requires planning, effort, and persistence over many years and even generations. In this chapter, we'll begin to outline how missions work develops over time.

The Missions Cycle

Fruitful missions is a self-perpetuating process. We see this on an individual level in the Bible. When Andrew discovered the Messiah, he brought others to know him. This happened in Philippi as well. The Philippian jailer came to faith in Christ and, as a result, so did his entire household (Acts 16:31–34). This is the nature of life. It grows and reproduces.

The same phenomenon occurs at the level of the church. Healthy churches lead to more healthy churches. Students of missions have often spoken of this in terms of the missions cycle. We can trace the main elements of a missions cycle in Paul's work in Philippi. Paul's team, led by Barnabas originally, was sent out by the church at Antioch (Acts 13:2ff.). Paul is sent from Antioch a second time (15:36–41). Later Paul received the Macedonian call, and they soon traveled to Philippi (16:1–13). They began evangelizing, and Lydia and others were converted (16:14–21). They built up the new believers, and a church was formed. I'm not sure how long they were in Philippi, but Paul would return on two or three more occasions (20:1–2, 6; 1 Tim. 1:3). Of course, he wrote the letter to the Philippians to help further establish them in their faith. They would have also received copies of the apostle's other circular letters. Paul also used the church at Philippi as a launching point for further missionary travels, and the church gladly participated in this process by sending its own emissaries to minister to him. As a result, other churches were planted in Greece.

Perhaps the simplest form of the cycle is this:

1. A missionary is sent
2. The missionary evangelizes.
3. A church is formed as people are converted.
4. In the new church, potential new missionaries are identified and trained.
5. New missionaries are sent out.

In our ministry, we've boiled it down to four steps:

1. Send.
2. Establish a ministry center.
3. Start a church.
4. Train.

Ministry centers represent an accepted platform for growing the ministry. It may take the form of a weekly Bible

Study, activities in a community center, Sunday services in someone's home, an after-school program, or any number of settings where the community is regularly engaged.

Of course, it's possible to break this down in more complex ways. David Hesselgrave makes a convincing case that Paul employed a ten-step cycle.[16] The International Mission Board (IMB) of the Southern Baptist Convention describes their process in a way that is essentially a missionary cycle consisting of "six core, reproducing tasks":[17]

1. **Entry**. We gain access to a people, begin to learn their language, and seek to understand their culture.

2. **Evangelism**. We intentionally cross barriers to share the gospel in ways that are meaningful with both individuals and groups of people.

3. **Discipleship**. We teach believers how to obey all the commandments of God so that they grow in understanding, character, and godly behavior.

4. **Healthy Church Formation**. We help organize disciples into churches that bear the characteristics of health described in the Bible.

5. **Leadership Development**. We help new churches identify, equip, and appoint leaders and church multipliers.

---

[16] David Hesselgrave, *Planting Churches Cross-Culturally: North America and Beyond* (Grand Rapids: Baker Academic, 2000).

[17] "Church Planting," International Mission Board, https://www.imb.org/missions-church-planting/

6. **Exit**. We believe new churches have the responsibility to join in the spread of the gospel throughout the world. We look for churches that demonstrate multiple generations of disciple-making and church growth and that are ready to send their own missionaries to proclaim the gospel among unreached peoples and places.

This is an helpful and concise description of the process. Of course, I can't resist tinkering with it a bit. I'd like to add a few things. First, I think it's good to include the vital element of prayer. I know the IMB would agree. Prayer is an element that should undergird the entire process, so it makes sense for the sake of brevity to not include it as a specific step. However, given my personal tendency towards activism without prayer, I'd like to include it. I also think it would be good to add "sending" as a step in the process. Before a missionary can "enter" he must be sent. This is the job of the local church, and it should be built into the process. I might also prefer to include discipleship under "healthy church formation." I like the IMB's description of discipleship, and I think it strengthens the role of the church if we include it under "healthy church formation." By the same token, we might include leadership development under healthy church formation, but there is a case for leaving it as a separate step: effective leadership development often requires the support of third parties such as seminaries. I'd also change the final step from "exit" to "sending." For reasons I'll explain later,

I'm skeptical about the value of leaving. However, the IMB correctly emphasizes the ongoing nature of the cycle which results in the new churches sending their own missionaries. Where the conditions are right, a church planting movement can be encouraged.

So if I can modify the IMB's list, I'd propose a cycle that looks like this:

1. The church prays.
2. A missionary is sent out.
3. The missionary enters the target culture.
4. The missionary evangelizes.[18]
5. A church is formed as people are converted.
6. In the new church, potential new missionaries are identified and trained.
7. The church prays.
8. New missionaries are sent out.
9. A church planting movement is encouraged.

It might be broken down in other ways; I don't think there is some sort of canonical mission cycle. But my purpose here is to let you see the ongoing nature of the process. In the following pages, we'll describe the steps of this cycle in more detail.

---

[18] This is where the missionary would build a platform or ministry center if necessary.

Step 1: The Church Prays

The modern missionary movement began with prayer—a lot of it. In 1747, Jonathan Edwards finished a short work with a long title: *An Humble Attempt to Promote an Explicit Agreement and Visible Union of God's People thro' the World, in Extraordinary Prayer, for the Revival of Religion, and the Advancement of Christ's Kingdom on Earth, Pursuant to Scripture Promise and Prophecies Concerning the Last Time.* The work was written in support of an idea proposed by Scottish ministers in 1744 to institute a "Concert of Prayer." This would consist of special seasons of prayer in churches and prayer societies for the "extraordinary applications to the God of all grace" for the revival of "true religion in all parts of Christendom, and to deliver all nations from their great and manifold spiritual calamities and miseries, and bless them with the unspeakable benefits of the kingdom of our glorious Redeemer, and fill the whole earth with his glory."

Almost forty years after Edwards published his *Humble Attempt*, it was republished by a Baptist Pastor, John Sutcliff, from the English Midlands. In 1784, Concerts of Prayer began among English Baptists. Slowly, events began to unfold which led to the modern missionary movement. In this out-of-the-way part of England, a revival gradually broke out among the pastors and churches of the Northamptonshire Association of Baptist Churches. One of these pastors, Andrew Fuller, published a groundbreaking work, *The Gospel Worthy of all Acceptation*. In 1786, Fuller's friend, Carey was ordained. Another pastor of the Northamptonshire Association, John Ryland, described a meeting from this time in his journal:

> Brethren Fuller, Sutcliff, Carey, and I, kept this day as a private fast, in my study: read the Epistles to Timothy and Titus . . . and each prayed twice—Carey with singular enlargement and pungency. Our chief design was to implore a revival of godliness in our own souls, in our churches, and in the church at large.[19]

It wasn't until 1792 that Carey's *Enquiry* was published and the Baptist Missionary Society founded. In January of the following year, Carey was approved as the first BMS missionary. He sailed for India in June of 1793. By that time, nearly fifty years had passed since the original call to prayer had been issued by the ministers in Scotland. Carey had written in the *Enquiry*:

> One of the first, and most important of those duties which are incumbent upon us, is fervent and united prayer. However the

---

[19] Michael A. G. Haykin, *One Heart and One Soul: John Sutcliff of Olney, His Friends and His Times* (England: Evangelical Press, 1994), 169.

influence of the Holy Spirit may be set at nought, and run down by many, it will be found upon trial, that all means which we can use, without it, will be ineffectual. If a temple is raised for God in the heathen world, it will not be by might, nor by power, nor by the authority of the magistrate, or the eloquence of the orator; but by my Spirit, saith the Lord of Hosts. We must therefore be in real earnest in supplicating his blessing upon our labours.

Notice that while Carey places great emphasis on prayer, he assumes that prayer leads to "labours." In another place he would write, "If you want the kingdom of God speeded go out and speed it yourselves; only obedience rationalizes prayer: only missions redeem your intercessions from insincerity."

Step 2: A Missionary Is Sent out

Earlier we emphasized the critical role the sending church plays in sending out missionaries. It's the church's responsibility to provide a healthy model that can be reproduced on the field. But it's also its responsibility of the sending church to make sure the missionary it sends out is an adequate candidate. (We've already mentioned the book *The Master Plan of Evangelism*. This book outlines the approach Jesus used in preparing his disciples for worldwide ministry.) Paul's approach seems to mirror that of Jesus. In 2 Timothy 2:2 he writes, "and what you have heard from me in the presence of many witnesses entrust to faithful men, who will be able to teach others also." Paul looked for young men of proven character, and then he brought them along as he planted churches. They were trained on the road. In the following pages, we'll break this process down a bit by looking at the example of Carey.

When the pastors of the Northamptonshire Baptist Association voted to organize the Particular Baptist Missionary Society, they took two practical steps that are essential for beginning a missionary endeavor. In a fine example of the use of available means, they took up an offering in Fuller's snuff box. They also began to look for their first missionary. They actually chose two. John Thomas, a Baptist who they did not know well but who had the advantage of having spent time in India, and Carey. Thomas proved to be a gadfly, though he was used by the Lord. Carey, on the other hand, would set the pattern for future missionaries with his inspired and faithful ministry, in spite of a marital relationship that would most likely disqualify him today.

Carey possessed four qualities that a missionary today should also possess: calling, character, gifting, and experience.

1. Calling. Carey had a clear sense of calling that was evident to the other pastors of the Northamptonshire Association. Paul provides a New Testament

example. Paul knew clearly the Lord had a mission for him. This was confirmed by his fruitfulness in ministry and the guidance the Holy Spirit gave the church in Antioch Acts 13. A clear sense of calling is an enormous benefit when things are difficult on the field.

2. Character. Carey would often regret the lack of integrity of some of the men who were sent to help him in India. Paul and Barnabas had a sharp disagreement about the suitability of John Mark for the missionary task. The issue at the heart of their dispute was the character of Mark. They disagreed about Mark, but not about the importance of character. Have you noticed that in 2 Timothy 2:2, Paul doesn't speak of experience or academic credentials? He calls for men of faithful character. Missionary work requires men (and women) of proven character. No one is perfect, but it's the church's responsibility to be sure that under the pressure of missionary work the candidate will have the character to see the course. Missionaries require an enduring character coupled with great flexibility. Not soft, and yet not brittle.

3. Gifting. Not everyone is cut out for missionary work. Can you learn another language? Can you learn to speak it well? It might come as a surprise

that learning to speak a foreign language fluently is much more difficult (and at times more humiliating) than getting a good grade in biblical Greek in seminary. Are you good enough with people to learn their culture well enough to pastor them? Are you sufficiently entrepreneurial to start a new ministry and flexible enough to fit into a team on the field that may consist of national leaders and workers that think about things in a very different way from your own? If the strategy includes something like business as mission, there are other qualities to consider. And then can you come back to the States and transition back into American culture—and don't forget American church culture—long enough to raise support or project monies without getting overly frustrated with those who don't have the benefit of all that you've seen and learned? Some of this should become evident in a well-executed internship process in the sending church. Carey had given evidence of his gifting before he went to the field. He was a passionate and gifted student of not just the Scriptures, but of the world and its languages long before he wrote the *Enquiry*.

4. Experience. Carey also had the benefit of pastoral experience. He had led two churches, first in Moulton and then in Leicester. In both cases, he healed serious divisions and set the church on a

path to significant growth. The challenges of learning a new language and culture are sufficient for a missionary's first term. He should already have had enough actual ministry experience at home so that both he and his sending church know that God has and will use him to bring about spiritual change in the life of others.

In addition to evaluating the candidate and preparing him for the field, the sending process requires that the sending church take responsibility for the financial support of the missionary on the field. Since the days of Carey, the picture of a miner going down into a pit has served as an analogy of the relationship between the missionary and those who send them. Carey and the pastors of the Northamptonshire Association were familiar with coal mining and its inherent dangers. These pastors made the commitment to hold the rope if Carey would go down into the pit. Sending a missionary involves taking responsibility for his family's well-being both financially, emotionally, and spiritually. This is an enormous responsibility and shouldn't be taken on lightly. And the burden shouldn't be turned over to third parties. Churches should certainly seek partnerships with church associations and missions organizations. And the missionary should be willing to travel and raise support. But the sending church should never sit back and let others carry most of the weight. They should be aggressively proactive in helping their missionary reach an appropriate level of support to live and work on the field. There are sufficient causes for worry on the field. The missionary also shouldn't have the added burden of worrying about shaky support base.

In Philippians, Paul commends the believers there for the efforts they've made to support his ministry. They sent an offering which Paul considered a "fragrant offering, a sacrifice acceptable and pleasing to the Lord" (Phil. 4:18). In addition, they had sent Epaphroditus not only to bring the offering, but to minister personally to Paul.

The final issue I'd like to mention under the discussion of "sending" is how to decide *where* to send a missionary. Many factors must be weighed. Sometimes a missionary will have a strong sense of calling and attraction to a specific field or ministry. This should be taken into serious consideration even if it's not always decisive. Carey had a deep interest in the islands of Polynesia before providential circumstances led him to India.

The decision-making process can be so complex it would be a challenge to the processing power of a super-computer. How do you bring together all of the elements of field, language, culture, support, family, team, missions agency, and more?

Let me briefly describe how my wife and I ended up on the field. It was a conjunction of a personal sense of calling, providential circumstances, and wise counsel. Above all, there was a good process that allowed us to hear the guidance of the Holy Spirit. Providentially, doors opened for us to be sent out under the Baptist mission board my parents were with. We had been in serving in the church in Miami for about four years when I began to question whether it was time to go to the field. I approached the pastor, and he was open but suggested we pull together a group of men in the church to pray. It was a great experience. We prayed for a month. When we met again, I wasn't sure what the answer would be, but I felt peace about the process. The consensus was that it wasn't quite yet time. To be honest, I wasn't disappointed. It felt like clear guidance from the Lord.

After this, we were in the church another three years or so. These years were actually more fruitful than the preceding years. I was able to work for a Christian college during this time which gave me experience that has been useful on the field. We started the English ministry in the church (remember it was a Spanish church). This was a great experience. Even though the ministry didn't grow large at that time, it did give me the confidence that we could start something from scratch. During that time God also brought into the church a woman who would eventually join us on the field in Argentina. We would've never met her had we left. She has been a critical member of the team in Argentina for more than twenty years. In other words, the three years weren't wasted time.   Eventually, I begin to feel the tug of the field again, and I approached the pastor about whether it might be time. Again we prayed, and this time the answer was "go." We never regretted the years we spent in Miami. The blessings that accrued to us at that time became multiplying factors in the years to come. None of the time was wasted.

Here's the bottom line on decision making. With a submissive heart, seek the will of the Lord in the context of wise counselors, and he'll guide and bless you.

Step 3: The Missionary Enters the Target culture

The next step in the missionary cycle is entering the target culture. In the old days, missionaries went by ship. In the days of sail, this could take months. In most cases, the new missionary family would have never been overseas before. When my parents went to the field in 1972, we took a cargo ship from the port of Houston and spent almost five weeks at sea. The ship had room for twelve passengers, six of which were our family. It was an Argentine ship, and the sailors and stewards gave us our first experience of Argentine culture.

Nowadays, air travel is much more efficient. Ideally, a family will be able to make at least one survey trip to the field before they move permanently. There are many good practical reasons for this. You can see firsthand what houses or apartments are like and make inquiries about what household items should be shipped. You can meet future team members. And it gives you the opportunity to begin the process of getting to know to the new culture. This may help reduce the potential effect of culture shock.

The sending church should be aware the first several months on the field may be among the most difficult in a missionary's life. The first blush of romance can often give way to frustration. Language study is often a trying experience. The new missionary, perhaps with an advanced degree, discovers that on the field they're reduced to the vocabulary of a small child. Cultural differences are often opaque to an outsider and challenging to learn. Usually, the children pick up the language more quickly, but at times they also suffer in the transition. Decisions about children's education are the most difficult a missionary must make.

Language studies require at least two years of intensive effort. There are no shortcuts in this process. Missionaries who don't acquire fluency will always be limited in their ministry. Wise sending churches will encourage their missionaries to dedicate sufficient time to the process. Both the missionary and the sending church must avoid the temptation to feel that nothing has been accomplished unless the missionary can point to number of conversions or a work started during the first term. While the Lord may give spiritual fruit even in this early period, the goal must be to acquire the language, culture, and get to know the country.

Permanent decisions about where to start a first church, or which team to join, or which ministry to start are usually best left for late in the first term on the field. First impressions in a new country are often not the best on which to make long-term strategic decisions. These decisions are best taken after a period of exploring the country and an extended process of prayer. Ideally, the sending church and other stakeholders will visit the field during the latter stages of the first term to provide a sounding board for the missionary as he begins to make long-term ministry decisions.

The first term on the field is also a critical time to evaluate team relationships. Core team relationships are often one of the most significant factors in missionary attrition. Missionaries can find themselves thrown into a relationship with another missionary with whom there is little compatibility. The team relationship can over the years become as close as a family, so it's essential that there be a correct fit. Part of this simply requires a growing maturity on the part of the missionaries. All relationships require self-sacrifice and a Christlike spirit. At the same time, it's wise to not make final commitments until the end of the first term. Of course, the process may vary depending on the structure on the field of the particular missions sending agency.

When my parents went to the field missionaries served for terms of four years on the field and returned to the States for a year-long furlough. This cycle marked the missionaries career. Nowadays, with the ease of air travel, this has begun to change. Returning to the States for an entire year is often not healthy for the work on the field. Besides, it's expensive to rent a house and purchase a car for a year in the U.S. Whatever the case, it's usually good for a missionary to stay on the field for a first term of anywhere from two-and-a-half to four years. This is often enough time to make progress in the language, begin to learn the culture and make decisions about long term ministry direction. The greatest temptation is to shortchange this process. Both missionary and sending church should understand that the first term lays the indispensable foundation for everything that follows.

Step 4: The Missionary Evangelizes

The next step in the process, assuming you aren't joining a team with projects already in place, is to begin evangelistic efforts. During our second term on the field we did a lot of evangelism. We made friends in our neighborhood through the kids' school. I took a class at the university to meet people. I also served on the PTA of our children's school. We rented a location downtown in an area that has several square blocks closed off to vehicle traffic. Thousands of people from all over the city walk through this part of the city every day. We passed out thousands upon thousands of pieces of literature, including gospel tracts and invitations to films and conferences we organized.

To be honest, I can't think of a single thing that was extraordinarily successful. We showed a film once in a large plaza downtown and had 600 people sign cards expressing interest in receiving further information. We did the follow-up, but as best we could tell, none ever came to church.

Nonetheless, as we persisted, we began to see fruit. In some cases, it was just one person coming to the gospel film or conference and who then made a profession of faith and began to grow. We started to notice a pattern. Nothing we ever did produced significant results. However, we came to the conclusion that we should continue evangelizing as best we could because often, after an event, we'd see fruit that came to us from an unexpected direction. It was as if the Lord was saying to us, "I am glad you're evangelizing, but I want to make sure that you don't think that the fruit is the result of your efforts or your clever ideas."

Our sending church, and other churches, helped in those first years by sending teams to help with evangelism. Spanish speakers were welcome, but many English speakers came as well and did important work helping us canvas neighborhoods, hand out invitations and organize evangelistic events.

Looking back, I think two things set us on the path of long-term growth. The first was the generous businessman from the U.S. who helped us purchase a building near downtown. This gave us the needed space and the sense of permanence that comes with having a place of your own to hang a sign. The second thing was that after the initial phases of evangelism, as we began to disciple new converts, they began to bring in friends and family. In other words, the centrifugal missions process jump-started the centripetal process. New converts became the most persuasive arguments for the gospel as their lives changed from darkness to light.

At this point, I want to mention that early in the church planting process, before a church has launched, it may be strategically helpful to start what I call a ministry center.

In the early days of modern missions, one strategy was to establish a missions station. In India, Carey and his team set up many such stations which consisted of a European missionary working with Indian evangelists and pastors. Often a school was begun since Indian parents wanted their children to learn to read. This provided contacts for the gospel and had the added benefit of producing a generation of literate young people who could read the scriptures. A similar strategy often works today. In La Rinconada, for example, we built a house for the church planter and a church building that they used to provide tutoring to children who needed help to do well in school.

In some places, some sort of platform is essential. If you're called to serve in many parts of the 10/40 window, the only way to gain access is through a small business, or as a teacher, or as a tentmaker. The right platform can provide opportunities to build relationships and share Christ. The wrong platform can mean more problems than it's worth. One of the difficulties of business as mission is that important decisions have to be made before the missionary arrives on the field. Such projects serve in much the same way as a ministry center as a vehicle for bringing the missionary into contact with the people, but it's more complicated. The church and missionary will want to do all they can to get expert advice before launching a project. The practice of business as mission is still in its infant phase and there is much to learn.

Step 5: A Church Is Formed as People Are Converted

A church doesn't spring up overnight. I think it should be understood that a church is more than a group of people who happen to gather for a Bible study. As a Reformed Baptist, I believe that a critical threshold is when people sign a mutual covenant affirming their doctrinal commitment and their willingness to live in a church relationship under the authority of Scripture. Ideally, the group should have a pastor, and even better, an additional elder or two.

Iglesia Crecer was formed by signing a church covenant on August 24, 1997. It had a pastor, but since it was me, I wouldn't want to make too much of that. Those first couple of years were joyful. The group often met in our home, and we did a lot of individual discipleship. There were problems, but the issues were those of young Christians learning to walk. The church consisted mainly of young couples and college-age students. It really felt like a big youth group.

A couple of years in, my wife and I had a strange experience. The church had grown to maybe forty in attendance. By that time there were older couples who had joined, and there were a few older children. My wife and I looked at each other and at the same time said, "This is a real church!" I don't know what it was that caused that simultaneous reaction. It was a subjective thing, and I don't offer it as some sort of ecclesiological litmus test. (I wouldn't say, "Your church is a church when you suddenly have the sensation that it is a church.") But the reason this experience has stuck in my mind is that it's similar to an experience I've had raising children. I remember at different stages looking at one or other of my children and thinking, "Where did this little human come from?" I also remember having periods of anxiety about the church. I guess since it wasn't obvious what had brought the church into existence I worried that it could just as well fall apart. I couldn't take our efforts and add them up in a way that mathematically produced a church. Relief came when I accepted the obvious fact that I hadn't given life to the church—God had. And I couldn't preserve the church, but God would.

These brief paragraphs don't constitute a manual on cross-cultural church planting. During the early days, we emphasized a few key ideas that are still important to us. We wanted to have an emphasis on sound doctrine and expository preaching. But we wanted this focus to be tempered by love. As I've already mentioned, we adopted Ephesians 4:15 as our theme verse: "Rather, speaking the truth in love, we are to grow up in every way into him who is the head, into Christ." We also placed a great deal of emphasis on the Great Commission.

The church grew out of a small group that was based on close communion around the God's Word. The church had—and to a great degree still has—a strong family feel. As the church grew, we worked to give it ecclesiological shape. But it's essential to understand that in a healthy church, communion precedes polity. Where church life is based on that communion and around the Word, it's not difficult to shape the church with biblical polity. But polity can easily be abstracted from actual body life. Where a punctilious approach to polity is the driving force, a church will not grow. You might produce an interesting historical diorama that would grace a church history museum, but not a living, breathing church.

In the next chapter, we'll continue exploring this process of sending out missionaries that eventually, through much prayer and God's leadership, leads to a church planting movement.

CHAPTER 6

Extending the Missions Cycle

n the last chapter, we provided a brief overview of the missionary cycle up to the point of planting a church on the field. It might well seem that this is the end goal of the process, but it's not. The goal is to see churches on the field become self-supporting, self-governing and self-replicating. In some ways, the first church plant is just the beginning. The real work is still ahead. It is similar to the difference between building a house and building a city. The job is orders of magnitude larger.

Step 6: New Missionaries Are Identified and Trained

The first church plant is of critical importance because it becomes a model of all future churches and the base from which new missionaries are sent out. There are many things involved in shaping the new church that we'll skip over. The principles that need to be taught and worked out in the life of the church are laid out in many of the excellent books published by 9Marks.[20]

From here on, each point in the cycle except for the last one is in some ways a repetition of a previous point. This point is about faithful men and women who respond to God's call. Like every other point, this one has a special relationship to the point about prayer. I explained earlier how before I went to the mission field I had read Coleman's book on the *Master Plan of Evangelism*. The book inspired me to begin asking the Lord for twelve men we could work with. Many years later, looking back, I can say the Lord has answered that prayer many times over.

We've already looked at the point Paul made in 2 Timothy 2:2, "and what you have heard from me in the presence of many witnesses entrust to faithful men, who will be able to teach others also." As we've seen, this verse emphasizes character. We know that Jesus's disciples were far from perfect. But where there is a willing heart, character can be developed with the Holy Spirit's help.

In missions, character is of primary importance. When Carey was asked to what he attributed his fruitfulness, he said that he knew how to plod. We might say he was a

---

[20] See Mark Dever, *9 Marks of a Healthy Church*, 3rd ed. (Wheaton, IL: Crossway, 2013); Mark Dever, *The Deliberate Church: Building Your Ministry on the Gospel* (Wheaton, IL: Crossway, 2005). Visit http://www.9marks.org for more resources.

visionary; that he was remarkably courageous; or that he was gifted in languages. But Carey attributed his success to simple plodding. Plodding is evidence not of talent, but of character. It's a type of courage based on hope that has been forged by God in the fires of experience.

Another emphasis of 2 Timothy 2:2 is the generational nature of the missionary task. It's like a long relay race where one generation passes the baton to the next. Each generation is responsible for running as hard and as long as possible, but it must also ensure that the following generation doesn't miss the exchange. The handoff is critical.

Carey and his colleagues placed great emphasis on raising up Indian pastors and evangelists. They were impressed with their potential and understood that they could in many ways exceed the original missionaries in their effectiveness. Carey, for example, said the best gospel sermon in Bengali he ever heard was preached by Krishna Pal. Carey and partners expressed their commitment to developing local leaders, writing in the Serampore Compact, "Another part of our work is the forming our native brethren to usefulness, fostering every kind of genius, and cherishing every gift and grace in them. In this respect we can scarcely be too lavish of our attention to their improvement. It is only by means of native preachers that we can hope for the universal spread of the gospel throughout this immense continent."[21]

---

[21] In 1800, the missionaries associated with William Carey signed this covenant which committed them to a series of missiological principles which are still relevant today. It was authored by William Ward, but it is representative of Carey's thinking.

In my teenage years, I at times encountered prejudice among a few missionaries towards Argentines. I always thought this was absurd. Some of the most brilliant people I had ever met were Latin Americans. My dad felt the same frustration at times. I remember him telling me something an older missionary from Mexico had told him, "You must remember that the same Holy Spirit that lives in us, lives in them."

One of my biggest concerns has been the inadequate resources for training leaders in Latin America and elsewhere. Only recently has the introduction of online technologies allowed the delivery of top quality theological instruction to students in Spanish on a large scale. There is still an abysmal deficit in institutions that maintain the highest academic standards side-by-side with a firm commitment to conservative, confessional theology.

At Seminario Bíblico William Carey we're committed to raising up a generation of pastors and missionary scholars who will provide a foundation for Hispanic theological education in the future. I'm not sure missions supporters always understand the importance of these efforts. We sometimes run into the same sort of frustrating incomprehension that Carey experienced when they founded Serampore College. To me, the logic is quite clear. My Argentine colleagues are as gifted as I am both spiritually and intellectually. In fact, the case could easily be made that they're *more* gifted. My calling isn't superior to theirs, and my responsibility under the divine command of the Great Commission isn't greater.

Given these facts, why shouldn't they have access to training and education as good as what I received at Reformed Theological Seminary and the Southern Baptist Theological Seminary?

Having said this, not all leaders need a seminary-level education. In our work in Argentina, we've worked with the idea that every leader needs his or her own critical path of development. Some should study theology at the highest level, others just need a well-rounded grounding in Bible, theology, and ministry skills. The critical path will vary depending on the individual's calling and life circumstances. Many pastors who've been laboring years need someone to come beside them with practical resources to help with the issues they face in ministry on a day-to-day basis. Regardless, everyone needs to maintain a focus on character development.

Step 7: The Churches Pray

In the second prayer stage in the missionary cycle, a resonance effect is created between the prayers of the original sending church and the new church plant. I don't know how you could measure the effect, but it seems to me that the same prayers repeated by the members of a mother and daughter church must be beneficial. For this to happen, there must be a level of intentional effort on the part of both churches to stay synchronized in their missions purpose and the prayers that flow from that mission. This is important since it's possible for both the sending church and the daughter church to experience mission drift.

Historically, there has been a tendency of missionaries in some environments to drift from sound doctrine. Often, the missionary has the best of intentions and is attempting to find effective ways of reaching people on their field. We know some earlier generations of missionaries have fallen prey to liberalism. In our current environment, in some situations, missionaries have succumbed to the dangers of relativism found in multiculturalism and postmodernism. The result has been to water down the gospel and reduce the church to the lowest common denominator. It's vital that sending churches stay close to their missionaries to help guard against doctrinal drift. Of course, this requires the wisdom to distinguish legitimate attempts to enculturate the mission.

Just as missionaries can drift, so too can sending and supporting churches. This can take various forms. In some circles, I've seen an increasing self-centeredness. The church focuses on its own growth to the exclusion of world missions. In these situations, often there is a preference for short-term projects with a big, quick emotional payoff and little long-term commitment. In other circles, there has been a tendency to manufacture theological disagreements that are mostly irrelevant to the missions work on the field and then force the missionary to take sides with inevitable consequences for the missionary's support.

Whatever the case, a periodic trip by the leaders of a

sending church to visit the work on the field is as just as important as having the missionary return to report on occasion. It's a great joy for a sending church to pray alongside a daughter church as the new church takes its own first steps in fulfilling its missions responsibilities.

Step 8: New Missionaries Are Sent Out

The missionary process involves evangelizing and planting churches in areas equivalent to Jerusalem, Judea, Samaria, and the uttermost parts of the earth. In our case this has meant planting in the city of Córdoba, in other communities near the city of Córdoba such as Malvinas, Saldán and Jesús Maria, then in more remote areas of our province such as La Rinconada and Villa Dolores, and in the far north of Argentina in Cachi in the province of Salta in an area that is culturally different from Córdoba. At this point we're working with a dozen church plants in Argentina. In addition, we've sent short-term missionaries to Africa, and we have a missionary from our church in a country in Southeast Asia.

It may not be exactly clear which of these works is a true missionary work. In other words, at what point is a geographical and cultural barrier large enough to say this isn't just a church plant, but a missions church plant? This may be arbitrary, but we've considered the works in the far north of the province of Córdoba and the work in the far north of Argentina to be mission works. The cultures in these areas are different from the city of Córdoba, and the hardship involved in establishing the work has been considerable even if there's not a significant language barrier.

Even if all of the works planted around the city are not actually mission works, they are certainly part of the missions sending process. We're in the process of beginning an association of churches with all of the works that have come out of the original church in Córdoba. The purpose of this association of churches is primarily to coordinate efforts for raising support and sending out new church planters and missionaries. While it's also a purpose of the association to provide fellowship for the pastors and their churches, I have a quirky idea that the best sort of fellowship isn't fellowship for fellowship sake, but fellowship around a shared purpose that extends beyond our own needs. That's why I'm convinced a new church plant should, from day one, support other new church plants and foreign missions. We should always see our ministry as one link in an ever-lengthening chain and not as the terminal link.

One of the purposes of the new association is for the churches to begin to provide mutual support and for the influence of the mother church in Córdoba to decrease eventually. While its initial role of providing a model and serving as a resource center for the new church plants is of great importance, over the long-term, it's essential that the original church in Córdoba become one of many sister churches.

We're beginning the process of sending missionaries overseas. We have much to learn. The logistics involved in maintaining missionaries in a foreign country, especially on another continent, are often complicated. We recognize that our institutional knowledge is limited, so we may seek partnerships with international missions agencies. The challenges of sending missionaries from countries in Latin America are complicated by unique factors. For example, a recent devaluation of the *peso* meant that the support we were sending to our missionary in Southeast Asia lost half of its value overnight. Up to this point, our policy had been that our missionaries should be supported by the offerings of Argentine churches. I continue to think this is the best policy for the pastors and missionaries we support within Argentina, and even nearby countries. But for missionaries further afield it may not be practical.

At this stage, we'll probably be looking to place our missionaries on existing international teams. But as time goes along, if the Lord permits, we'll form our own teams. There are different ways to approach team formation. In Córdoba, the process has been incremental. Our first term we worked closely with my parents, but we planned to start an independent work our second term. In our case, the process has been organic. Those who joined our team have brought unique gifts to the table and have shared a sense of ownership of this work. Those who've joined the team had gotten to know us and the work before coming on board. They've all sensed a personal sense of calling to the role they now fill.

It's possible to pull together a new team from people

who've never really known each other previously, but this is more difficult. Where this is the case, it seems to me it's important to have clear leadership structures in place. Ideally, the senior roles should be filled by people with proven experience.

Step 9: A Church Planting Movement Is Encouraged

Earlier we looked at a church planting cycle put forward by the IMB. This cycle is an excellent expression of missions thinking. I really had only one quibble with it. The last point is, "Exit. We believe new churches have the responsibility to join in the spread of the gospel throughout the world. We look for churches that demonstrate multiple generations of disciple-making and church growth and that are ready to send their own missionaries to proclaim the gospel among unreached peoples and places." The only disagreement I have with this paragraph is the first word, "exit." I agree that as a church planting movement matures it needs to become independent—self-governing and self-replicating. The role of the foreign missionary will change. But who says we should leave?

I think there is as much danger from a hurried departure as there is from a missionary who overstays his welcome. I've seen missionaries leave immature works after two years because they labored under the idea that, given the indigenous principle, if they stayed longer they were no longer missionaries. The result is a work that struggles needlessly or dies. I'm also aware of seminaries that became breeding grounds for false doctrine because support from a U.S. denomination dried up before there was a solid transition plan in place.

The indigenous principle is a valid rule of thumb for missions work, but like a lot of other missions principles, it needs to be applied with a certain amount of common sense. Let me give you an example. For some years our church supported an Argentine doctor who ran a medical clinic in third world country on a different continent. He's a great guy, and he and his team have done good work. I respect him. He always talked to us about the need for non-medical personnel to do discipleship work with the people because the medical work absorbed so much time. We sent people to help on a short-term basis. However, we decided to not go further with the partnership because he felt uncomfortable with the idea of planting a church. He had come into the country under the sponsorship of a local association of churches. He would tell us that the level of teaching in those churches was abysmal and that some of the leaders were actually corrupt. But he didn't feel he could plant a church because this association wouldn't approve. Personally, I think this is taking the indigenous principle too far.

So what's my point? As became evident in the last point—step 8 and now step 9—at this stage of the process we've moved from thinking in terms of planting one church to creating a church planting movement. This is no time to "exit." It's time for roles to change, but not for people to leave. It's much like the growth of a family. I don't boss my adult children around, but I'm still there to advise and encourage.

My wife and I have realized that we've entered the grandparent phase of ministry. We don't do most of the work anymore. I'm fine not changing diapers. In fact, I don't feel like I really know what is going on most of the time on an operational level. The control freak in me struggles with this at times, but the Lord has raised up competent leaders to fill many roles. More and more our job is to coach and cheerlead. But we don't have any plans to leave.

My dad died on the field and is buried just outside of the city. I've never heard an Argentine say, he stayed too long. Instead, they're grateful that he was so committed to the people of this country that he refused to retire and return to the States. Here's the thing: If you spend a lifetime first ministering to, and then alongside a group of brethren, a spiritual relationship develops that transcends national identities. I don't think that Paul ever thought, "I need to retire so that the original Jewish leadership of the church can be replaced by Gentiles." Rather he wrote, "My desire is to depart and be with Christ, for that is far better. But to remain in the flesh is more necessary on your account" (Phil. 1:23–24).

I understand that on a case-by-case basis, there are many legitimate reasons for a missionary to change fields or return to the States. My concern is with strategic decisions that are guided more by abstract missiological principles than by common sense and the understanding that relationships on the field are between members of a spiritual family. The thing is, creating a genuine church planting movement is a multigenerational endeavor. Premature withdrawal from the field can hamper the process.

I'm a little leery of using the phrase "church planting movement" since, in some contexts, what is meant isn't particularly healthy. The idea of church planting movements can go wrong when missionaries, through an understandable desire to accelerate the process, end up taking invalid shortcuts. The result is that sometimes important things are reduced to their lowest common denominator—a Bible study is classified as a church, and an enthusiastic new believer is considered a pastor. The homogeneous unit approach to church planting has been justified precisely on the basis that it's easier to plant churches quickly where people aren't forced to cross cultural barriers that make them uncomfortable. This may speed up the process in the short term, but it's harmful over the long term. Church planting is a spiritual process, and there are specific spiritual dynamics, which really can't be accelerated. Spiritual maturity in the life of a believer or the life of the church can be helped along by solid teaching and loving discipleship. But in the end, the pace of growth depends on the Holy Spirit and not us.

Because of these negative connotations, I prefer to think in terms of the church association and not a church planting movement. But to be clear, the purpose of an association is to promote the planting of churches near and far. A healthy church association requires a commitment to a doctoral standard. How can we walk together unless we agreed? At the same time, I'm also convinced that where the mere maintenance of a doctoral standard is the central purpose of the association, the most likely result is stagnation and ironically, even division as theological hairsplitting develops. A healthy association will be centered on preaching the gospel and planting churches.

The opposite danger must also be guarded against. While an association of churches should be centered on missions outreach, there is always the temptation to water down foundational standards for the expedient of faster growth. I'm not sure how you avoid driving into one ditch or the other over the long term. As crucial as clear foundational documents are, ultimately the critical factor is the character of each generation of leaders—which takes us back to 2 Timothy 2:2.

Associations of churches exist to encourage and facilitate the planting of churches both at home and abroad. An association can help coordinate resources and foster mutual accountability. As a Baptist, I think that the association shouldn't take authority over the individual congregations, but it can support the ongoing church cycle in at least two principal ways: the theological education of its workers and the continuing logistical support of those workers once they've begun planting churches. This requires secondary organizations, such as missions agencies, to provide logistical support for church planters and foreign missionaries. On the field, the construction of church buildings also requires some sort of agency. And of course, seminaries and Bible institutes are needed to train pastors.

At this point, we've moved well beyond the initial stages of missions outreach. We've gone from discussing how an individual church can send a missionary to plant another church to a discussion of developing denominational machinery on the field. Let me insist that this is part of the responsible missions work even if it raises many questions. We've hinted at these questions already, but we will delve into them a little deeper in an appendix to this book.

The Secret of Growth

The last few chapters have been about the hard work of missions. We've just skimmed over the surface of the issues involved. Entire books could be written about subjects such as Bible translation or Christian literature. Or about financing missions work. Or about church planting itself in a cross-cultural context. God has chosen to work through us and our limited capabilities. However, beyond all the necessary discussions of tools or logistics, we need to remember the life is in the seed. In other words, the Word, not us.

The work is often slow. We dream of revival and work for it, but much of missions depends on faithful plodding. Since Carey went to India in 1792 Protestant Christianity has become a worldwide religion, no longer limited to northern

Europe and the American colonies. This has been the fruit of many thousands of uncelebrated missionaries and those faithful supporters who sent them.

I know a missionary in Africa who told me about a visit he made to a graveyard at an old missions station from the 19th century. As he looked at the names on the gravestones, he realized he was reading a chronicle of many missionaries who had left home and who had soon died from tropical diseases not long after arrival. I've always wondered about the sense of calling it would take to get on a ship to Africa to replace a missionary who had died of disease a short time after replacing another missionary who had also died of disease.

All of those who dedicate their lives to the cause of world missions, whether sent ones or senders, stand on the shoulders of those who've gone before. I long to see Christ honored as hundreds of healthy churches are planted in places where the gospel message has yet to take deep root. I'm open to new ideas and five-year plans, but what we most need are men and women who are committed to a lifetime of plodding.

CHAPTER 7

Engaging Your Church in Missions

L et me tell you a secret: Missionaries hate raising support. There are a few blessed souls who are gifted fundraisers and thrive on it, but most of us hate it. The process can be grueling, and most missionaries have deputation war stories to tell. I could tell you about the blizzard we drove through in South Dakota. Or the time the front tire blew out and caught fire on the old motorhome we traveled in for a year.

In spite of the misadventures, it's also true that there were many moments of blessing on deputation. I have vivid memories of times in the motor home like when our kids caught sight of the statue of liberty as we drove past New York. Or how nervous my wife was when I decided it was a good idea to drive through Manhattan in the motor home (it was fine, really). I remember standing on the top of a mountain we climbed in Idaho, and the time we stayed in a trailer park with a big statue of Yogi Bear.

I also remember all of the churches that took us in after long hours on the highway.

Some of those churches still support us. We're overwhelmed at times thinking of churches that have supported us faithfully for so long. My wife and I have received monthly support from a church in Hutchinson, Kansas, since we became missionaries more than twenty-five years ago. Every so often we receive a letter from, a senior citizen who is a member of that church. We don't know much about her, but we remember meeting her. And we remember she promised to pray for us. Her occasional letters show familiarity with everything we have ever written in our prayer updates. It's clear that for a quarter of a century she has never forgotten her promise to pray.

I was never an especially good fundraiser, but the Lord has always been faithful, and he has raised up many friends of the work over the years. Beyond the issue of my personal limitations, I think we're going through a transition in missions support models on the macro level. In general, it seems more difficult to raise support among churches. This is due to many factors. There has been a generational shift away from the long-term monthly support that is the bread and butter of missionaries on the field. It's more difficult to get your ministry before a church. Fewer and fewer churches have annual missions conferences. I understand why. Churches are struggling to adapt to the hectic lifestyle of their members and who has time to come to church every night for a week? Please don't hear a note of cynicism here. We struggle with the same issues in our church.

Older models of missions support weren't perfect. My parents had over a hundred supporting churches because, when they went out, churches liked to have as many missionaries as possible that they supported at $10 a month. A shift took place when many saw that it would be better for a church to support just a few missionaries with significant monthly contributions. This rightly allows for better accountability and fellowship between the church and its missionaries. The downside is that it's more difficult to get into those churches that are committed to the substantial support of a few. If your home church doesn't support you in that way, the process can be uphill.

As a result of these factors, missionaries are relying more and more on raising support from individuals. I think individual support is an important part of the mix, but if it becomes the primary means, it inevitably reduces the missionary's accountability to the churches. I don't know what the solution is other than to pray for a missions revival in the hearts of God's people. There may be some top-down remedies that can be applied at the denominational or missions agency level, but what we most need is for the Holy Spirit to create a seller's market.

What do I mean by a "seller's market" in missions support? For my entire missions career, there has been a buyer's market. In other words, the missionary offers his life for service on the mission field, and it's his job to convince churches that he's a worthy candidate, that he'll get the job done, and that the church should financially back him. There are a lot of missionaries, and the church can afford to be selective. So the missionary has to sell himself the church. As a rule, churches don't seek out the missionary. Instead, the missionary is responsible for networking and marketing himself to the churches.

I wonder what would happen if churches started to suspect that their investment portfolio in missions might be evaluated on the day of judgment? It might create a seller's market. Maybe churches would begin to look for good missionaries to support. Maybe pastors would cold call lists of missionaries. Maybe missions committees would approach qualified missionaries with PowerPoint presentations, and videos about their church and its desire to buy in. I know this sounds weird, but pay attention to Paul's words to the believers in Philippi:

> And you Philippians yourselves know that in the beginning of the gospel, when I left Macedonia, no church entered into partnership with me in giving and receiving, except you only. Even in Thessalonica you sent me help for my needs once and again. Not that I seek the gift, but I seek the fruit that increases to your credit. (Phil. 4:15–17)

Did you ever think, "I wish I had invested in Apple, or Microsoft when they first went public?" Let me whisper some inside information in your ear: Your investment in global missions will pay eternal dividends of incalculable worth. In a sense, our structural problems with missions support is that of supply and demand. If the demand for opportunities to support missionaries and missions projects increased, a lot of issues with various support models would sort themselves out. If you've read this far into this book, then I'm preaching to the choir. You're already onboard. So I invite you to do the one thing that can work: prayer for a missions revival in our churches.

The Support Crisis

I believe there is a general crisis in missions support models. Missions giving is dropping in some denominations, and there has been a generational shift in attitudes towards world missions. There is an increasing interest in supporting projects with a quick bang for the buck. Especially if it's a social project. This isn't always a bad thing, but it does mean it's more difficult to find the long-term support that keeps a missionary on the field year after year.

In our case, raising support has always been a challenge. It took us several years to get our support to a sustainable level, and we've never had large amounts of personal support to invest in the work itself. Thankfully, this hasn't placed significant limitations on the work for two reasons.

First, the people of our church, Iglesia Crecer in Córdoba have given generously to missions and church planting projects. Second, several years ago we began The Crecer Foundation to raise funds for infrastructure such as property, building, and funding for the seminary. The purpose of the foundation was to provide financing at strategic points in the church planting cycle in a way that would not create unhealthy dependency.

Our mission board does a great job of providing monthly financial services and such things as health insurance. It can even lend a small amount of money for a church building, but not in the amounts necessary for a church to purchase property in a 21st-century metropolitan area. The amounts available might help build a tin roof church on the Amazon river, but they're not adequate for a work in the city.

I don't offer this as a criticism. Our missions agency does a professional job and has been of enormous help to us over the years. The problem lies with the model. And it's not limited to any one agency; rather, these sort of problems exist in various manifestations across the gamut of missions organizations.

I don't have a grand solution to offer. To be quite honest, I'm skeptical of worldwide master plans. I think the best solutions will come from below as individual churches take on the responsibility of world missions. It's possible to fall prey to the fatal conceit of centralized control in missions just as in economics. The world is too big, and conditions vary widely from field to field that it's best to be skeptical of technocratic missiological approaches that look at the world as if it were a giant chess board.

Let me explain it like this. We're involved at the time of this writing in over a dozen church plants at different stages of maturity in Argentina. Every situation is unique. While various general principles apply across the board, the concrete reality of each is different. As a lead elder of the church in Córdoba, I'm not the authority on the situation in La Rinconada. The church planter on the ground is the true authority. I try to offer general advice and encouragement, but he's the expert. There are analogical situations, but ultimately, each ministry is unique. If this is the case when we compare works within Argentina, how much more is it true when we compare works from different countries or continents?

My brother was a master gunnery sergeant, the highest enlisted rank in the United States Marine Corps. One thing you learn is that even officers are respectful to master gunnery sergeants. The Marines have a doctrine that I always thought should be applied to missions work. It's called "the strategic corporal." The Marine Corps is suspicious of an over-reliance on centralized control, and they empower their non-commissioned officers to make critical decisions at the front. This is because the situation in battle is fluid and it's essential to make the right decision quickly and not after a lengthy bureaucratic process of communication up and back down the chain of command. This doesn't mean that the non-commissioned officer is isolated from the rest of the force. He is plugged into a network and receives information from multiple nodes including units on the ground and in the air. This is why the Marines place heavy emphasis on training and preparation. Because the non-commissioned officer makes critical decisions. And it's why the Marines win.

So I hope that the next wave of missions will feature highly prepared multinational missions teams backed by an active, plugged-in sending church and a handful of other partner churches. These teams will be connected with more extensive networks of support that might include missions boards and specialized parachurch organizations and even businesses where a business as mission project is in view. Mission agencies will offer advice and support, but the initiative will flow from the close interaction of the team on the field and the sending church.

Traditional missions organizations still have an essential role to play, but developments in technology make it feasible for the local church to become the primary missions agency. For a scenario like this to develop it will take not only dedicated missionaries but radically committed local churches. Next, let's look at what it will take for your church to step up to the challenge.

1. Pastors Should Lead

It would be easy to blame our current crisis in missions support on millennials or their younger counterparts, but

I'm not buying it. While I recognize that there are characteristics common to each generation, I think the whole idea of what we might call "generational essentialism" is a bit overdone. One's "generation" no more determines the destiny of an individual than the fact that I was born in the Chinese year of the ox.

William Carey faced even more significant obstacles to launching a missions program than we do. Much is made of the opposition he faced from certain pastors to his ideas. What is not as well known is that Carey was part of a group of several younger pastors who were concerned about the apathy they saw in their denomination. There would've been no Carey if not for the leadership of young pastors like Andrew Fuller, John Sutcliff, John Ryland, and Samuel Pearce. Just as in Carey's day, our current missions crisis will be solved by the leadership of young pastors who want to see our churches get serious about missions.

Among evangelicals, for quite a while now there has been a tendency to attempt to build churches by catering to the perceived needs of those we would like to see in the pews. This really amounts to forfeiting pastoral leadership. The role of the church is to glorify God and speak to human needs as they are defined by Scripture. What people need is the gospel, and the gospel should be worked into every area of people's lives. In our world where everything has lost a sense of significance, we can show people how to live their lives for something of eternal value. One of the greatest things we can do for our people is to paint the picture of

God's cosmic plan to redeem all of creation and to glorify his Son. Then we can show them how their church is part of that plan and that as members, so are they. It's the responsibility of pastors to connect those dots.

Pastors signal what is important by what they preach, and by what they become involved in personally and visibly. If a church respects their pastor and sees him as a capable leader, his involvement in missions is critical. It is not enough to delegate missions to a committee. It's not enough to have the secretary hang occasional prayer letters on the bulletin board in the foyer. Pastors must engage visibly. They must be advocates for missions and the missionary before their congregation. They need to go on a mission trip themselves. They may need to help their people overcome fears of traveling abroad or guide them in arranging financial priorities to free them up to make investments in God's kingdom. Missionary churches are the fruit of missionary pastors.

2. Churches Must Pray

In previous chapters, we talked about the critical role of prayer in missions. It's essential for churches to work missionary prayer into every aspect of church life. These prayers should be both broad and specific. Broad like Jonathan Edwards's call to prayer for the advancement of Christ's kingdom on earth. But then they should focus in on specific projects and needs. There are numerous ways of receiving updates on efforts around the world. For example, your denomination probably publishes regular updates about its missionaries. Of course, when you support your own missionaries, you'll want to have a special focus on their ministries and lives. It's also good to pray for God to guide the church by providing new openings and for faithfulness in the commitments already assumed. Make the missions prayer ministry visible through your church's bulletins and social media. Pastors should model prayer for missions and missionaries in their services. Bottom line: just do it. Pray for God to stir your hearts for the nations. Pray for him to demolish obstacles that impede the progress of the gospel. Pray that the Word would have free course and the missionaries might be given utterance by the Spirit. Do it regularly and insistently. And then get ready for God to answer because he will. Above and beyond all that you hope because he intends to glorify his Son.

3. Missions Should Be Taught

The Bible is a missionary book, and it should be taught as such. It doesn't mean that every single message or lesson needs to be about missions, but it's easy to fail to make appropriate links to missions. Consider that every single epistle in the New Testament was written in the context of missions work. We should teach our people that missions is a major biblical, theological theme that runs from one end of scripture to the other. And our people need to sense the weight of the eschatological imperative of the Great

Commission. The great commission is reiterated in different forms in each of the gospels and the book of Acts. How can we make them feel the weight of it until we have felt it ourselves?

Pastors and teachers should be sensitive to the missional nature of Scripture and should preach and teach missions whenever they encounter it in the text—not just on special "mission emphasis" occasions. It would also be good to teach the history of the missionary expansion of the church and acquaint them with the biographies of leading missionaries such as David Brainerd, William Carey, and Adoniram Judson. People tend to imitate those who are held up as models.

4. Engage Your Congregation

Prayer and teaching are the spiritual drivers of missions in the church, but it's also essential to create channels of communication that keep missions and missionaries before the people. We also need to give people clear opportunities to get involved. Here are some ways to communicate with the church's membership:

- Give away missions books.
- Dedicate at least one page on your church website to define missions and explain how members can get involved.
- Promote short-term missions trips online, from the pulpit, and throughout your small groups.

- Make the missionary families visible throughout your church building. Leverage pictures, videos, and newsletters to increase awareness.
- If you offer an online giving web portal, make missions one of your top giving categories.
- If your church has an app, include pictures and information about your missionaries to encourage ongoing prayer.
- Talk about missions as you receive the offering each week. Share prayer requests from the field and praise reports as much as possible. Help church members understand why it is so important to give to missions. Have special times of prayer and fasting for your missionary families.

A missions communications strategy should be aimed at actually Involving your congregation in the support and practice of missions. Here are some ways for people to take their firsts steps:

- Ask missionaries to preach at your church when they visit the U.S.
- Celebrate missionaries by preparing for their arrival before visiting your church.
- Ask families to serve as host homes to care for missionary families.
- On a rotating basis, assign your missionaries to a small group that will communicate with them, pray

for them and even raise an offering to meet a specific ministry need.

- Get your entire church involved by hosting missionary preview events and giving your people an opportunity to connect with missionary families and ask questions. Make it a party. Have food, desserts, and coffee for people to spend more time in conversation.

- Have your missionary families spend time with one or more small groups or Sunday School classes to share their stories and build relationships with your people.

- Host an annual missions week and invite at least two to three missionary families to speak and engage your congregation.

As interest grows, missions trips provide the next step of involvement:

- Plan at least two adult missions trips per year.

- Plan survey trips to introduce adults in your congregation to missions.

- Challenge your church regularly to "go" and make a difference in the life and ministry of a missionary family.

- Don't just go to places that are cheap. Some fields are hard to get to. You may not be able to send thirty teens, but two or three influencers can go and come back with a report.

And it's important to start young:

- Plan at least one summer missions trip per year with a group of young people in your church.
- Plan activities and events to help them work for their trip and build their character in the process.
- Get parents involved early in the process and talk about the long-term benefits of developing a global perspective for their children's spiritual, professional, and relational development.[22]

5. Network for the Cause of Missions

An individual congregation can have a profound impact in a specific place, but to do so, it must seek partnerships on a variety of levels. The first place to look might best be one's own denomination. Groups like the Southern Baptist Convention and the Presbyterian Church in America have well-developed missions sending agencies. These agencies can provide a wealth of advice and resources and have an irreplaceable institutional knowledge.

Of course, there are other good organizations. Not everyone who is fit for the mission field is the right candidate

---

[22] Thanks to Marcel Sánchez at Global Church in Miami for his creative help with this section.

for every organization. Some agencies specialize in particular areas of the world or outreach to specific types of people groups. Some specialize in specific kinds of ministries such as translation work or providing professors for seminaries overseas.

There are also organizations that fill important narrow niches. In Argentina, we've been working closely with 9Marks which, while not a missions organization per se, provides resources and training to help churches develop a healthy polity. We've also begun to work with the Simeon Trust which offers training in expository preaching.[23] Both of these dovetail neatly with the instruction we provide through our seminary, Seminario Bíblico William Carey. Seminario Carey has benefitted from an articulation agreement with the Southern Baptist Theological Seminary. We also work closely with Poeima,[24] a publisher in Spanish that is doing an excellent job, and Coalición por el Evangelio (the sister organization of The Gospel Coalition) which provides great online material in Spanish and has done much to encourage a reformation of sound theology in our part of the world.[25]

Here are three things to look for when considering a partnership with an agency or organization:

---

[23] The Simeon Trusts exists to "promote the growth of the gospel of Jesus Christ throughout the world by training up the next generation of biblical expositors." https://simeontrust.org

[24] https://poiema.co/

[25] https://www.coalicionporelevangelio.org/

1. Prioritize personal relationships with specific missionaries and involvement in specific projects. The Philippians were motivated to give, not just to the general cause of world missions, but to the particular needs of Paul with whom they had a warm relationship.

2. Look for organizations that engage the missions task at one or more points along the church planting cycle.

3. Look for organizations that maximize the involvement of your people. This might mean trips to the field, but it certainly means directed prayer.

Whatever the case, work at building solid partnerships with existing organizations. The Crecer Foundation is looking for enduring partnerships with a handful of churches that would be interested in engaging their people in different ways at different points on the church planting cycle. We have opportunities available at each step of the process. Of course, we are not the only group that needs partners. In fact, we might not be the best for your congregation. This takes us back to the importance of prayer. God will guide you into those partnerships where the gifts of your church can be most fruitfully employed.

Beyond partnering with established organizations, it is also good to look for informal networking opportunities. A lot can be accomplished by purposefully seeking out others who might be interested in supporting a missions project.

A church that wants to send a missionary of its own would be wise to look for good missionaries from other churches to support at a generous level. While it might be good to provide 100 percent of your missionary's support if your church is able, I'm not sure this is the best approach. It's generally healthier for the sending church to provide a significant percentage of support and for a handful of other churches to make up the difference. If for no other reason, this allows churches which don't have a missionary of their own, to invest in the cause of world missions.

There are many viable configurations of churches, agencies, and organizations for sending and supporting missionaries on the field. The critical point I want to get across is the importance of the sending church in the process. The sending church is the final authority and the ultimate source of accountability. This implies that the sending church must take a proactive role in networking and raising the support of the missionaries it sends or supports. The local church should be the motor of world missions.

6. Send and Support Missionaries

By sending I mean playing the role of mother church for a missionary or missions project. Sending churches should continuously cultivate personal relationships with field workers and aim to be an integral part of their ministries and a consistent blessing to their lives. The sending church provides training, accountability, and makes a significant commitment to the overall support of a missionary or project. A good sending church will do more than provide support. It'll be an advocate for the missionary and proactively look for new sources of support or resources. It'll defend the cause of the missionary on the field. It'll have the missionary's back. In other words, it's the primary rope holder. In the modern era of jet travel, this means the leaders and members of churches should visit the field to make themselves familiar with the needs of their missionary, and they should return home to mobilize support for the work.

A supporting church may take on a similar role although the primary lines of accountability will run through the sending church. For a church that is just starting to get serious about missions, the role of supporting church is a good one. It doesn't require the same level of engagement although even in this role the church should strive to offer maximal support. Supporting churches should engage in personal relationships with field workers and aim to be an integral part of their ministries and a consistent blessing to their lives. The significant support model allows a church to build a more intimate relationship with a missionary and their work on the field. As I already mentioned, when my parents went to the field, many churches had the idea of supporting as many missionaries as possible at $10–20 dollars a month. This made true relationship and accountability impossible. If a missionary can raise support from just a handful of churches, the relationship can be much more involved with each one.

Providing Transformational-Level Support: A Case Study

Whether as a sending church, or a supporting church, it's good to look for opportunities to do more than provide monthly donations that help keep a missionary fed, pay his bills, and keep his kids in shoes. Monthly support is hugely important, of course, but I've been trying to paint a picture of an even more effective and rewarding level of involvement. We might call this "transformational-level support." Let me give you an example from our own ministry to illustrate what I mean.

Our sending church in Miami has been a critical part of our ministry since the beginning. They provided the training I described in an earlier chapter, and they have given us a generous amount of monthly support. In addition, they provide 100 percent of the single missionaries support who has been a key member of our team for more than twenty years. They've helped with numerous projects, sent teams to evangelize, and been an advocate for us in countless ways. We've also been blessed with significant support from five or six other churches. One of those churches is Mill Creek Community Church, in Shawnee, Kansas, which was started by a close friend of mine, Gary Pauley.

Mill Creek was a church plant out of a large church in Olathe, Kansas. They did things right and began with a core group of about 100 people. They never looked back from there. Gary had been a friend since my wife and I married.

He had gone to the same high school in Missouri as my wife. Gary and I had a lot in common, including a love for missions that had been fanned by contact with Rudy Johnson. Gary had gone on a mission trip to Peru when he was in high school. He had seriously considered missions as a career but ended up being a church planter. Nonetheless, missions was part of his genetic makeup.

Mill Creek took us on for support almost from its beginning. When our church in Córdoba was about a year old, they sent a mission team to help do some evangelism. At that time we were paying rent for our first location in downtown Córdoba. We didn't own a car, so I rode the trolley back and forth between downtown. One day, I had been on the trolley for just a few blocks when I felt the urge to get off and walk the rest of the way home. I took a slightly different route than usual and walked up Lima street. Just a few blocks from where we were meeting, I saw a building with a for sale sign on it. I had the strongest feeling we should look into buying this building.

The problem was that the building cost $100,000, and I couldn't lay my hands on even an extra $100. At that time, our personal support was really subsistence level. We couldn't afford to buy a car for several years. And our young congregation certainly didn't have the funds. What's more, in Argentina, as in most parts of the world, you can't walk into a bank and ask for a loan to buy a church building. I didn't know of another source of financing.

Still, we felt we should pray about it. When the team

from Mill Creek came down, I thought we should take them to see the building. The realtor gave us the keys, and we looked around. It needed a lot of work, but the team from Mill creek apparently had an imagination as outlandish as my own. They all had the same sense that I did—that this building was it. I knew they Mill Creek was a new church and I had no expectation they could help us in a significant way. So we stood in a patio at the back of the property as drizzling rain fell and we prayed. When we finished praying one of the team members said, "I wish my boss were here. He would write a check." I gave him my "that's nice" smile and thought to myself, "Yeah, right."

The first day this man was back at work he went to see his boss. He told him about the building and said, "If you had been there, you would have written a check for $100,000." So his boss wrote the check.

At first, it was a loan. We were to pay it back with monthly payments equivalent to the rent we had been paying. A couple of years into the process, the donor told me God had blessed his business, and he didn't need the money back. I said I was very grateful, but that for the sake of the church in Argentina we couldn't receive it as a gift. Instead, I proposed that we continue making payments into a revolving fund that would be used to help future church plants. At this stage, two decades later, the original investment has been recycled to help two additional churches buy property and build.

Gary made numerous trips to Argentina during those

years. He got to know the church planters who were working with us. When they felt called to go to Cachi, Mill Creek agreed to partner with us to get the new work off the ground. They sent a team down on a survey trip to Cachi before the church planters actually moved there. It was a great trip. The roads were a lot rougher back then, so it was more an adventure than it is now. I remember the small caravan of vehicles parked on the side of a mountain road looking at an indigenous altar high on the side of the canyon. This trip gave the team from Mill Creek a sense of the real needs in Cachi.

The church planters rented for the first couple years they were in Cachi and held meetings in their home. Their monthly support, including rent, came from the church in Córdoba. We still feel that our churches in Argentina should pay the salaries of their pastors without outside subsidies. But we had seen how strategic help with property could be the key factor in making a church plant viable.

In Cachi, there weren't many pieces of property available for purchase and those that were available were controlled by the city's mayor who was not friendly towards our efforts. One day, the church planter called me and told me that a local businessman had decided to sell a field on the edge of town and that if we hurried we could get a lot before they all sold or the mayor found out. Some people in our church in Córdoba put up the funds for one lot. Mill Creek Church sent us the money for another lot, and we quickly purchased two properties side by side.

Over the next few years, we built a house on the property for pastor's family to live in. Across the back of the property, in another stage of construction, we built a multipurpose building with a classroom, kitchen, bathrooms, and a room that will whole maybe eighty people on Sunday morning. There's still room on the property for a larger auditorium when the need arises.

During the first phase of construction, Mill Creek sent a team to work side-by-side with some of our people from Córdoba. Everyone from Córdoba who went on the trip still talks about how the American guys were working machines. Mill Creek also provided funding that matched offerings from the church in Córdoba. I think our church in Córdoba could've done the job by itself, but it would've only been half as big, and it would've taken twice as long.

The last time I was in Cachi, we had the meeting I described in an earlier chapter. I remember wishing Gary and the people from Mill Creek could be there to see what their generosity had produced. Almost ten years later, as their children played outside, thirty adults sat in a circle and told us of the joy and suffering they experienced as new followers of Christ. I think I can confidently paraphrase Paul to say that Mill Creek's gifts were a fragrant offering, a sacrifice acceptable to God. The result will be glory to our God and Father forever and ever. Amen (Phil. 4:18–20).

That is what I mean by transformational-level support. With a significant investment over a period of, say, five years, your church can be the key to planting a church somewhere in the world where the gospel is seldom heard. A few years of strenuous effort for an eternal harvest that glorifies Christ and fills us with unending joy.

Not every church is ready to tackle a transformational-level project—or send out their own missionary—but that doesn't mean you can't have an influence through partnerships. There are needs on the mission field right now that your church can meet, whatever your size. God in his providence will match your tools to a job that needs to be done. That's the way it works. Whatever your resources, Jesus will multiply them many times over.

Towards the end of the book of Philippians, Paul expressed deep affection for the members of that church: "Therefore, my brothers, whom I love and long for, my joy and my crown" (Phil. 4:1). All of his efforts and suffering had been worth it. Partnerships in the gospel produce a joy like no other.

Are you and your church ready to do missions?

The Crecer Foundation

I f you've finished this book, then it's possible that the Lord has you asking "What's next?" Perhaps you're a leader at a church and the thought of sending a team to an international location is daunting. Or you're the pastor of a small church and finding a healthy partnership on a different continent isn't something you have the bandwidth to accomplish. Or maybe your church has been a part of international missions for a number of years, but is now wanting to find ways to be more personally engaged.

I've mentioned The Crecer Foundation several times throughout the book, and would like to take a moment to explain who we are and what we do. As we explored earlier, churches are both the primary means and the primary end of the missionary task. Missionaries should be sent out, supported, and cared for by the local church. And as the Great Commission was given to the church and not to individuals, churches who don't have sent missionaries still have a responsibility to support and partner with missions work around the world. Of course, it helps to find tools and assistance for accomplishing God's mission. The Crecer Foundation works to provide these tools by creating partnerships between U.S. churches and Latin American ministries. Our mission isn't to hand out crutches or build one-sided relationships. We want to see proven Spanish-speaking leaders equipped to support kingdom growth around the world.

There are many ways these partnerships work, but first a reminder about why we so strongly value and support the work of leaders throughout Latin America.

The Problem

In global missions, the English-speaking church has often made two mistakes when taking the gospel to other countries.

First, there is the mistake of paternalism. North American churches often work as if it is their exclusive responsibility to spread the gospel. In regions like Latin America, we have, at times, been guilty of assuming a paternalistic role that, while well-intentioned, undermines true discipleship. The failure to see our Spanish-speaking brothers and sisters as full partners in the missionary enterprise has limited the growth of capable, national leaders and self-sufficient churches.

Second, there is the mistake of teaching an incomplete theology. Recognition of the first problem has produced an unhealthy pendulum swing. Political correctness has led to a failure to proclaim the Word in all its weightiness and to provide the same quality of theological training available in the United States. This too is a form of patronizing, and it deprives national leaders of the chance to grow into bold, Spirit-filled, Word-directed leaders. This in turn limits the potential of Latin American churches to disciple local communities and reach full strength as a force in global missions.

The Solution

In the Great Commission (Matt. 28:16–20), Christ sends his followers to the nations. He commands them to "make disciples," or empower others with the truth of the gospel, so that those individuals might go to the nations and make disciples themselves. Spanish-speaking leaders have the benefit of a lifetime of cultural insight which allows them to share the gospel with their respective communities in a way no foreign group could. Also, because of cultural factors, Latin Americans are uniquely suited for outreach to the Muslim world and other areas that are difficult for North Americans to reach. This leads us to a surprising conclusion. One of the most effective things we can do to reach the 10/40 window is support church planting and theological training in Latin America.

How can we be involved in international missions while still valuing the unique skills and leadership of those we serve? We focus our efforts on developing strategic partnerships between North American churches, organizations, and individuals who have a passion for kingdom-building in Latin America. These partnerships enable us to offer a wide variety of resources and logistical support. You'll see us working side-by-side with local leaders to give them additional resources for advancing their mission and the Kingdom of God. We're not the focal point of this story, but rather a partner who supports Spanish-speaking leaders, allowing them to grow and accelerate their respective ministries in a self-sufficient way.

Ministry Support Programs

In many areas throughout Latin America, pastors are extremely isolated, without the support or relationship of other biblical ministries to help them grow their church. To help fill this gap, we have several ministry support programs which allow local leaders to build trust and engage their communities. For example, in Argentine culture, the most difficult people to reach with the gospel are men. Missionaries have tried many strategies in small towns in Northern Argentina to reach men, but to no avail. Because of this we started escuelas de oficios—or trade schools.

Escuelas de oficios is all about bringing job training to people who don't have pathways to seek a better job. The the week-long schools are focused on teaching men for the purpose of reaching them with the gospel.

The classes taught are hands on and practical. This allows the Christian teachers to spend significant amounts of time with students, getting to know them well and gaining their trust. On the final day of the class, a clear presentation of the gospel is given, as well as a Bible for them to have in their household.

All ministry support programs are held in areas with a local church plant so that participants can connect with local churches and take steps in their spiritual lives.

Miguel lives in the desert of northern Córdoba, in a tiny town that struggles to get enough water, and doesn't have a religious foundation at all. His town is open to new faces but rarely experiences them. He was a recent participant in Crecer's Trade School program. In contrast to the hostility that missionaries in this area often face, the trade schools have seen overflowing classrooms. Men—and even some women—are eager to learn new labor skills that can bring them up to date in the workforce. The training goes hand in hand with relationship building, and always culminates with a gospel presentation.

The Crecer Foundation held a trade school workshop in Miguel's town of La Rinconada thanks to faithful stateside partners in Boise, who not only covered the costs but sent a team to be present and serve the community during the week of the school. Miguel had had some dealings with the local church plant but hadn't committed to a life for Christ yet.

During this week, he and the trade school leader developed a deep relationship. Long conversation led to Miguel's conversion and decision to be baptized. Miguel walked into the trade school hoping to learn new skills to provide for his family. He learned to weld, but he also walked out with a knowledge of Christ. Stateside partnerships with programs like this open doors financially and logistically where the Lord has already opened doors spiritually.

Long-Term Relationships

As I mentioned previously, our hope is to not simply dump money into a ministry and create a dependent relationship. While U.S. churches are blessed with vast financial resources compared to the rest of the world, all churches everywhere have a responsibility to lead their congregations to give sacrificially in the interest of kingdom growth. We've seen both U.S. based churches and Latin American church plants benefit greatly from committed, long-term relationships. You heard in chapter seven how a relationship like this pushed forward church planting efforts in Cachi, Argentina. Here is another example of kingdom growth through church partnerships.

First Baptist Church of Oak Grove, Missouri, knew they wanted to be involved with an overseas ministry for the long haul. They wanted to be part of another church's growth at the same time as their own church members grew. They began a partnership with the church plant in La Rinconada by giving offerings, sending teams for construction, and staying engaged with the local pastor. Over the course of 10 years, they were able to see how the church in La Rinconada grew, step by step, and they were able to get involved at important crossroads such as laying the foundation for a pastoral house, raising money for the new church building, and by sending a team to hang the ceiling of the church.

They've been able to develop a personal relationship with local Pastor Fabián and his wife Marcela, and see their babies grow into school kids. The joy of each new member and every step of progress at La Rinconada church is shared not only by the local congregation, but also by their faraway faith partners in Oak Grove. While Fabian and Marcela are able to encourage First Baptist in their commitment to missions, FBC Oak Grove are able to encourage Fabian and Marcela in their missionary work in La Rinconada.

Bret, one of the pastors in Oak Grove—the same team leader that came down on one of the first trips in 2008—led yet another trip in 2018, and was able to be an eyewitness to the growth that had taken place over ten years. He shared: "I started to say that I had seen the full cycle, but in reality it's not a cycle at all because God has much much more to do in this place!"

Short-Term Trips

Churches of any size should and can engage in international mission. It isn't simply a call to mid-sized or large churches, but all churches. Because of this, The Crecer Foundation coordinates short-term missions trips which support and encourage proven local leaders, helping them with projects that build trust with the community, evangelize the lost, and build up the church both spiritually and practically. Of course, the experience is often lifechanging for the the members of the US team.

The Crecer Foundation's partnerships with churches and seminaries in Latin America create a unique opportunity for the North American church to walk alongside and help equip Spanish-speaking leaders. We understand the logistical hurdle of sending teams internationally, so we organize your trip to fit the skills of your specific team. We work to keep costs low so that your fundraising efforts can have maximum impact in the lives of those you're serving. And once you are on the ground, we provide all in country transportation, lodging, guides, and translation so that you can be free to focus on helping the church planters you have partnered with.

We send teams to do a variety of work including:

- Building projects
- Door-to-door evangelism
- Children's festivals
- Trade workshops
- English talks
- Teen outreach
- Community aid

Amber is a college student from the United States who recently traveled to Condor Huasi, high in the Andes mountains of northwest Argentina. She came to Condor unprepared, not knowing of what lay ahead. However, God worked in her heart by teaching her that he is always in control. As a pastor's kid, Amber came from a background where she usually knew all the plans, but in Condor she didn't have that security.

The living situation in Condor was very different from Amber's American lifestyle, but it opened her eyes to how a significant portion of the world lives. Her team stayed with a couple who had to survive on subsistence level income from one day to the next. The people of Condor live difficult and isolated lives, but they need the gospel just as much as anyone else. Over the course of the week, Amber began to realize how real the Bible is for the people of Condor. The culture of Condor was very similar to the cultural experiences in the Bible. For example, the people of Condor herd sheep and bake bread. You can see how many of the stories in the Bible have immediate relevance.

Even though the people can easily relate to these aspects in the Bible, without people coming and explaining the Bible, the Condor people are still unreached (cf. Rom. 10:14–15). Amber's team worked alongside their Argentine teammates to make sure the gospel was heard throughout the valley.

Amber sums up her experience well: "I realized it took a combination of personalities and leadership abilities to give the gospel to the different families throughout the mountains. Along with observing, I had many opportunities to pray, really pray, in ways I had never done before. It took me going to the middle of nowhere in Argentina for me to learn the power of prayer. Praying for the people of Condor Huasi increased my burden for the lost and keeps me accountable to not let my

> experience in Condor stay in Condor, but go wherever I go. This trip grew my passion to share Jesus with my unsaved friends in the States and to the people I will encounter in the future.

The Crecer Foundation

Ultimately, we're simply servants, motivated, sustained, and empowered by God's Word to accomplish his mission his way. We desire to see the growth of Spanish-speaking leaders as they labor in places all around the world, preaching the gospel and planting churches. Will you partner with us? If you'd like to know more about how your church can actively engage in missions work through partnerships in Latin America, please visit **www.thecrecerfoundation.org** or email us at info@thecrecerfoundation.org.

Made in United States
Orlando, FL
06 February 2023